Around the World

A colourful atlas for kids

Illustrations by Christopher Corr

WeldonOwen
PUBLISHING

Contents

NORTH POLE
60

Greenland

Iceland

Scandinav

British
Isles

EUROPE
18

Canada

NORTH AMERICA
4

Pacific
Ocean

United states
of America

Atlantic
Ocean

North and
West Africa

Mexico

Caribbean
Islands

AFRICA
52

NORTH AMERICA 4
United States of America 6
Canada, Greenland and Iceland 7
Mexico and Central America...................8
Caribbean Islands 10

SOUTH AMERICA 12
Colombia, Ecuador, Peru and Venezuela..14
Brazil and northern South America..........15
Southern South America 16

Northern
South America

SOUTH AMERICA
12

EUROPE 18
Scandinavia 20
British Isles 21
Spain and Portugal 22
France, Andorra and Monaco 23
Netherlands, Belgium and Luxembourg 24
Germany, Switzerland, Liechtenstein
and Austria...25
North Central Europe 26
South Central Europe 27
Italy and Southern Europe.....................28
Albania, Greece and Macedonia............29
Baltic States and Russia 30

Southern
South
America

ASIA 32
Middle East 34
Central Asia 36
Afghanistan and Pakistan......................38
India and Southern Asia 39
Southeast Asia 40
China, Tibet, Mongolia and Taiwan........41
North and South Korea.........................42
Japan 43
Eastern Seas 44

Antarctica

SOUTH POLE
61

Arctic Ocean

Russia

Baltic states

Central Europe

ASIA 32

Central Asia

Middle East

Japan

China

Southern Asia

Southeast Asia

Pacific Ocean

East Africa

Eastern Seas

Central Africa

Indian Ocean

Pacific Islands

Southern Africa

Australia

OCEANIA 46

OCEANIA 46
Australia 48
Papua New Guinea and Solomon Islands 49
New Zealand and the Pacific 50

New Zealand

AFRICA 52
North and West Africa 54
Central Africa 56
East Africa 57
Southern Africa 58

POLAR REGIONS 60
North Pole 60
South Pole 61

WORLD MAP 62

INDEX/CREDITS 64

Southern Ocean

North America

North America is the third largest continent on Earth. It is made up of Canada, the United States of America (USA), Mexico, the islands of the Caribbean, the seven countries of Central America and Greenland, the world's largest island. Canada and the USA are the biggest countries by far. North America has snow-capped mountains, baking deserts, huge lakes and long rivers. It is also famous for its big, bustling cities, such as New York City and Mexico City.

Arctic Ocean

ALASKA (USA)

Pacific Ocean

Rocky Mountains

Hawaii (USA)

GREENLAND ICELAND

Hudson Bay

CANADA

UNITED STATES OF AMERICA

Atlantic Ocean

Gulf of Mexico

MEXICO

BAHAMAS

CUBA

HAITI

DOMINICAN REPUBLIC

JAMAICA

PUERTO RICO

VIRGIN ISLANDS

ANTIGUA & BARBUDA

ST KITTS & NEVIS

DOMINICA

ST LUCIA

BARBADOS

ST VINCENT & THE GRENADINES

GRENADA

TRINIDAD & TOBAGO

Caribbean Sea

BELIZE

GUATEMALA

EL SALVADOR

HONDURAS

NICARAGUA

COSTA RICA

PANAMA

United States of America

ALASKA

Humpback whale

Brown bear

Anchorage

Pacific Ocean

CANADA

Statue of Liberty
This huge statue is made from copper and stands in New York harbour. It is as tall as 25 adults. People can climb right up into the crown.

Moose

Mayflower

Niagara Falls

Bald eagle

CANADA

Native American

Washington, DC

New York city

Buffalo

Golden Gate Bridge

Mountain lion

Mt Rushmore

Rocky Mountains

UNITED STATES OF AMERICA

Baseball

Kentucky Derby

Wright Brothers' plane

Atlantic Ocean

HOLLYWOOD

Los Angeles

Jazz music

Grand Canyon
The Grand Canyon is a giant gash in Earth's surface. It was carved by water millions of years ago. It is nearly 2 kilometres (about 1 mile) deep.

Saguaro cactuses

Armadillo

MEXICO

Cowboys
Cowboys herd cows and other animals. They gallop after the cows on horseback and catch them by throwing long ropes, called lassos.

Gulf of Mexico

Manatee

CUBA

Pacific Ocean

HAWAII

Honolulu

Volcano

United states of America

How many faces are on Mt Rushmore?

The United States of America (USA) is a huge country, made up of 50 states. Most of the states are joined together, apart from Alaska and Hawaii. Alaska is in the far north, next to Canada. Hawaii, a group of islands in the Pacific Ocean, was formed by volcanoes.

More than 313 million people live in the USA. It is one of the richest and most powerful countries on Earth. Many people live in big, modern cities. The city of Los Angeles is famous for being the home of Hollywood, where many movie stars live.

Answer: Four

Canada, Greenland and Iceland

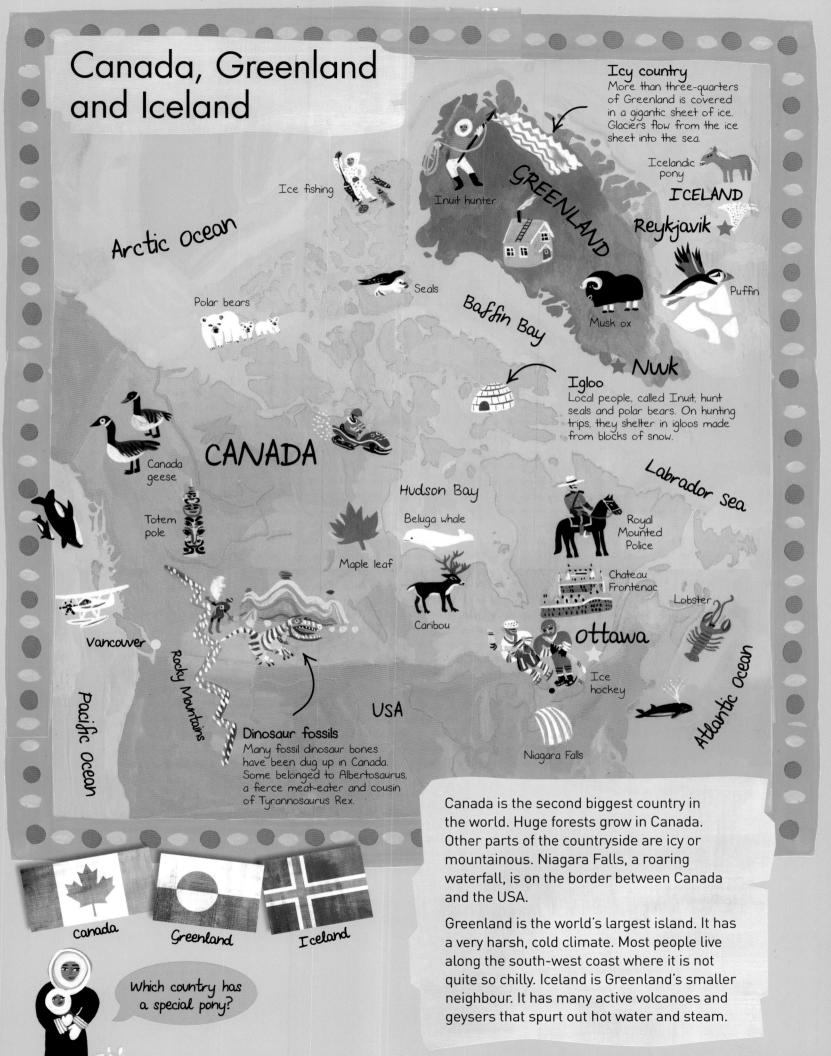

Icy country
More than three-quarters of Greenland is covered in a gigantic sheet of ice. Glaciers flow from the ice sheet into the sea.

Icelandic pony

GREENLAND

ICELAND

Reykjavik

Inuit hunter

Ice fishing

Arctic Ocean

Puffin

Seals

Baffin Bay

Musk ox

Polar bears

Nuuk

Igloo
Local people, called Inuit, hunt seals and polar bears. On hunting trips, they shelter in igloos made from blocks of snow.

CANADA

Canada geese

Totem pole

Hudson Bay

Beluga whale

Labrador sea

Royal Mounted Police

Maple leaf

Chateau Frontenac

Lobster

Caribou

Vancouver

Ottawa

Rocky Mountains

Ice hockey

USA

Pacific Ocean

Atlantic Ocean

Dinosaur fossils
Many fossil dinosaur bones have been dug up in Canada. Some belonged to Albertosaurus, a fierce meat-eater and cousin of Tyrannosaurus Rex.

Niagara Falls

Canada

Greenland

Iceland

Which country has a special pony?

Canada is the second biggest country in the world. Huge forests grow in Canada. Other parts of the countryside are icy or mountainous. Niagara Falls, a roaring waterfall, is on the border between Canada and the USA.

Greenland is the world's largest island. It has a very harsh, cold climate. Most people live along the south-west coast where it is not quite so chilly. Iceland is Greenland's smaller neighbour. It has many active volcanoes and geysers that spurt out hot water and steam.

Answer: Iceland

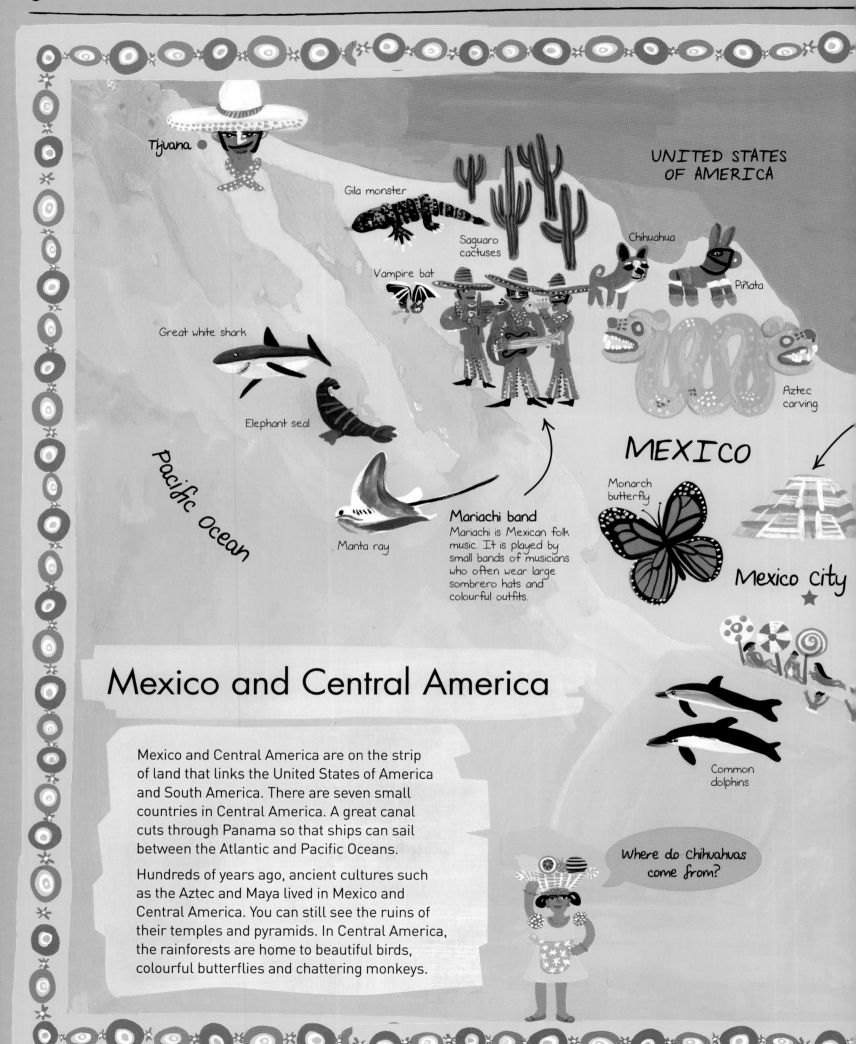

Tijuana

Gila monster

Saguaro cactuses

UNITED STATES OF AMERICA

Vampire bat

Chihuahua

Piñata

Great white shark

Aztec carving

Elephant seal

Pacific Ocean

MEXICO

Monarch butterfly

Manta ray

Mariachi band
Mariachi is Mexican folk music. It is played by small bands of musicians who often wear large sombrero hats and colourful outfits.

Mexico city

Common dolphins

Mexico and Central America

Mexico and Central America are on the strip of land that links the United States of America and South America. There are seven small countries in Central America. A great canal cuts through Panama so that ships can sail between the Atlantic and Pacific Oceans.

Hundreds of years ago, ancient cultures such as the Aztec and Maya lived in Mexico and Central America. You can still see the ruins of their temples and pyramids. In Central America, the rainforests are home to beautiful birds, colourful butterflies and chattering monkeys.

Where do Chihuahuas come from?

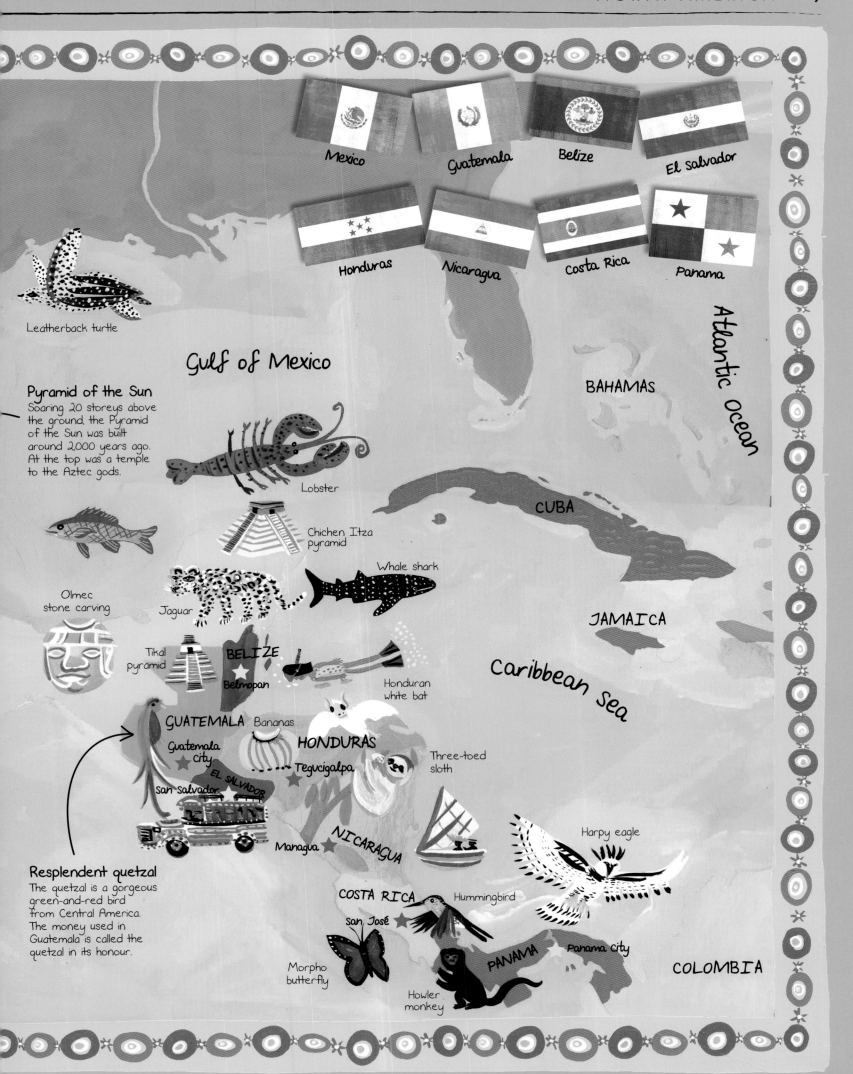

Mexico

Guatemala

Belize

El salvador

Honduras

Nicaragua

Costa Rica

Panama

Leatherback turtle

Gulf of Mexico

Pyramid of the Sun
Soaring 20 storeys above the ground, the Pyramid of the Sun was built around 2,000 years ago. At the top was a temple to the Aztec gods.

BAHAMAS

Atlantic Ocean

Lobster

Chichen Itza pyramid

CUBA

Olmec stone carving

Jaguar

Whale shark

JAMAICA

Tikal pyramid

BELIZE

Belmopan

Caribbean Sea

Honduran white bat

GUATEMALA   Bananas

HONDURAS

Guatemala city

Tegucigalpa

Three-toed sloth

EL SALVADOR

san salvador

NICARAGUA

Managua

Harpy eagle

Resplendent quetzal
The quetzal is a gorgeous green-and-red bird from Central America. The money used in Guatemala is called the quetzal in its honour.

COSTA RICA

Hummingbird

san José

Morpho butterfly

PANAMA

Panama city

Howler monkey

COLOMBIA

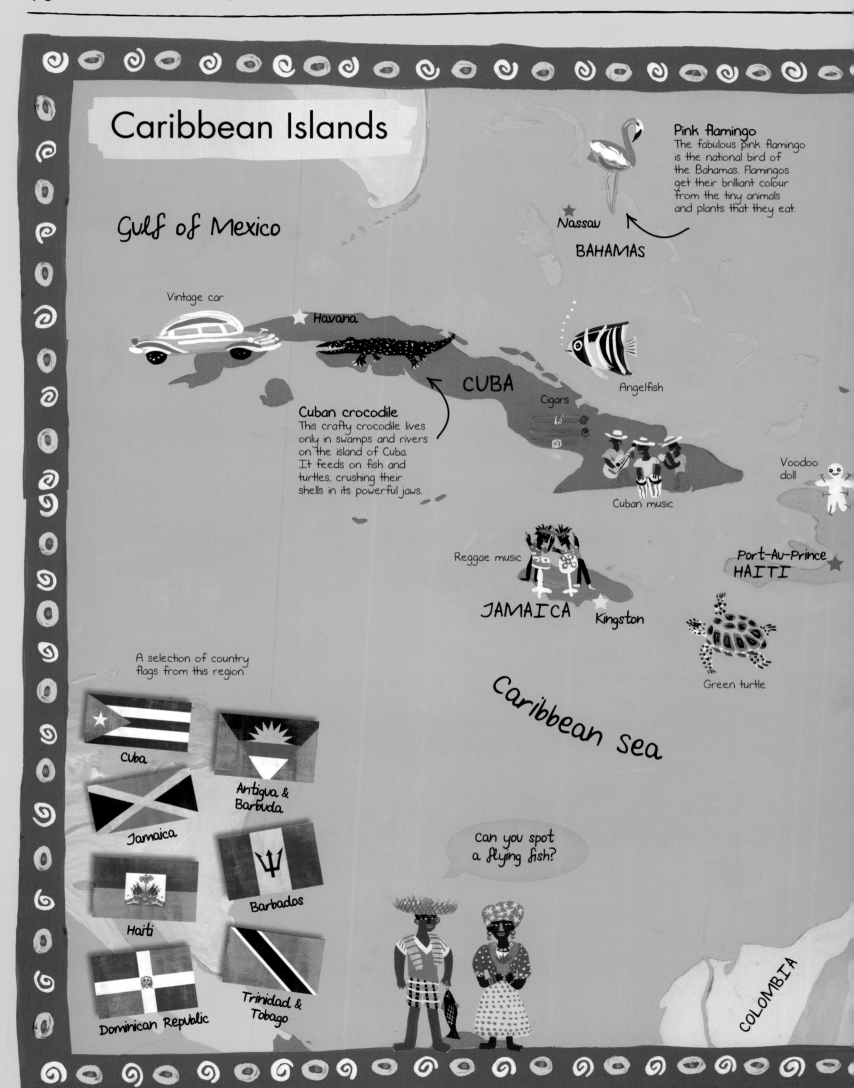

Caribbean Islands

Pink flamingo
The fabulous pink flamingo is the national bird of the Bahamas. Flamingos get their brilliant colour from the tiny animals and plants that they eat.

Gulf of Mexico

Nassau
BAHAMAS

Vintage car

★ Havana

CUBA

Angelfish

Cigars

Cuban crocodile
This crafty crocodile lives only in swamps and rivers on the island of Cuba. It feeds on fish and turtles, crushing their shells in its powerful jaws.

Cuban music

Voodoo doll

Reggae music

Port-Au-Prince
HAITI

JAMAICA   Kingston

Green turtle

A selection of country flags from this region

Caribbean Sea

Cuba

Antigua & Barbuda

Jamaica

Barbados

can you spot a flying fish?

Haiti

Dominican Republic

Trinidad & Tobago

COLOMBIA

Pirate ship
Hundreds of years ago, pirate ships prowled the Caribbean Sea on the lookout for treasure. On board were pirates, such as Blackbeard, who was famous for his fearsome looks.

To the east of Central America, hundreds of islands lie in the Caribbean Sea. The islands are known as the West Indies. Most of the large islands are also countries, including Jamaica, Barbados, Cuba and Trinidad & Tobago.

Each year, millions of tourists visit the islands to enjoy the sunny weather and sandy beaches. They swim in the warm sea and snorkel over the colourful coral reefs. But the islands can also be hit by fierce storms, called hurricanes, which bring howling winds and pouring rain.

Atlantic Ocean

Palm tree

Frigatebird

Scuba diver

DOMINICAN REPUBLIC

Solenodon

VIRGIN ISLANDS

Mango

Mongoose

Santo Domingo

San Juan
PUERTO RICO

ST KITTS & NEVIS

ANTIGUA & BARBUDA

Basseterre

St John's

Sail boat

Fishing boat

DOMINICA
Roseau

Sperm whale

Leatherback turtle

Castries
ST LUCIA

Cricket player

ST VINCENT & THE GRENADINES

Kingstown

Bridgetown
BARBADOS

Bananas

St George's GRENADA

Flying fish

Manta ray

Spices

Port-of-spain

Anaconda

VENEZUELA

TRINIDAD & TOBAGO

South America

The fourth largest continent, South America is home to almost 400 million people. It is made up of 12 countries. They include Brazil, Argentina and Peru. South America has some of the most spectacular scenery on Earth. The towering Andes mountains run all the way down the west side of the continent. To the east of the Andes is the Amazon Rainforest, the world's biggest rainforest.

BRAZIL

FRENCH GUIANA

SURINAME

GUYANA

VENEZUELA

COLOMBIA

ECUADOR

PERU

Andes

Galápagos Islands

Atlantic Ocean

PARAGUAY

URUGUAY

BOLIVIA

ARGENTINA

CHILE

Andes Mountains

Pacific Ocean

Colombia, Ecuador, Peru and Venezuela

PANAMA

Golden Mask
This mask from Colombia was made from a sheet of gold about 2,000 years ago. It was probably placed over a dead person's face before he was buried.

Poison-arrow frog

Red devils
Dressed in blood-red clothes and wearing devil masks, people dance through the streets to celebrate the festival of Corpus Christi in Venezuela.

★ Caracas

VENEZUELA

Lightning

Angel Falls

Bushmaster snake

Bogotá ★

Heliconia

BRAZIL

Andean condor

Quito ★

Playing pan pipes

COLOMBIA

ECUADOR

Amazon River

Machu Picchu
High in the Andes in Peru are the ruins of the ancient city of Machu Picchu. It was built by the Inca about 550 years ago, then mysteriously abandoned.

PERU

The countries of Colombia, Ecuador, Peru and Venezuela are at the north end of the Andes mountains. The mighty Amazon River begins high up in the mountains in Peru. The river flows an awesome 6,400 kilometres (4,000 miles) across the continent.

Venezuela is a country that has rich oil supplies. It also has the famous Angel Falls, the world's highest waterfall, which plunges 979 metres (3,212 feet) off a steep cliff. Off the coast of Ecuador lie the Galápagos Islands. They are home to some amazing animals, including giant tortoises and marine iguanas, that are not found anywhere else on Earth.

Llamas

Paddington Bear

Lima ★

Can you find the flag of Ecuador?

Andes Mountains

Sardines

BOLIVIA

Reed boat

Lake Titicaca

Ecuador

Peru

Venezuela

Colombia

VENEZUELA

Leatherback turtle

Georgetown
Paramaribo

Cayenne

GUYANA

SURINAME

FRENCH GUIANA

COLOMBIA

Cock-of-the-rock bird

Medicine man
A shaman is a wise man who is skilled in using rainforest plants as medicines. He passes on his knowledge to others in his tribe.

Angel Falls

Amazon River

Amazon River dolphin

Crocodiles

Amazon Rainforest
The Amazon Rainforest covers an area about the size of Australia. More kinds of animals live here than anywhere else in the world.

BRAZIL

Indigenous Kayapo

PERU

Poisonous snake

Carnival!
Every year, in February or March, it is carnival time in Rio de Janeiro. There are street parades with floats and dancers dressed in spectacular costumes.

Brasilia

Christ the Redeemer statue

BOLIVIA

Iguazu Falls

Samba music

Rio de Janeiro

Brazil and northern South America

Georgetown is the capital of which country?

Brazil is the largest country in South America and covers almost half of the continent. The might Amazon River flows through Brazil on its way to the sea. On its banks grows the Amazon rainforest, home to millions of animals and plants, and local peoples.

Guyana and Suriname are two of the smallest countries in South America. Only about 750,000 people live in Guyana, mostly along the coast. Suriname used to be ruled by the Netherlands. French Guiana is still governed by France.

Brazil

Guyana

Suriname

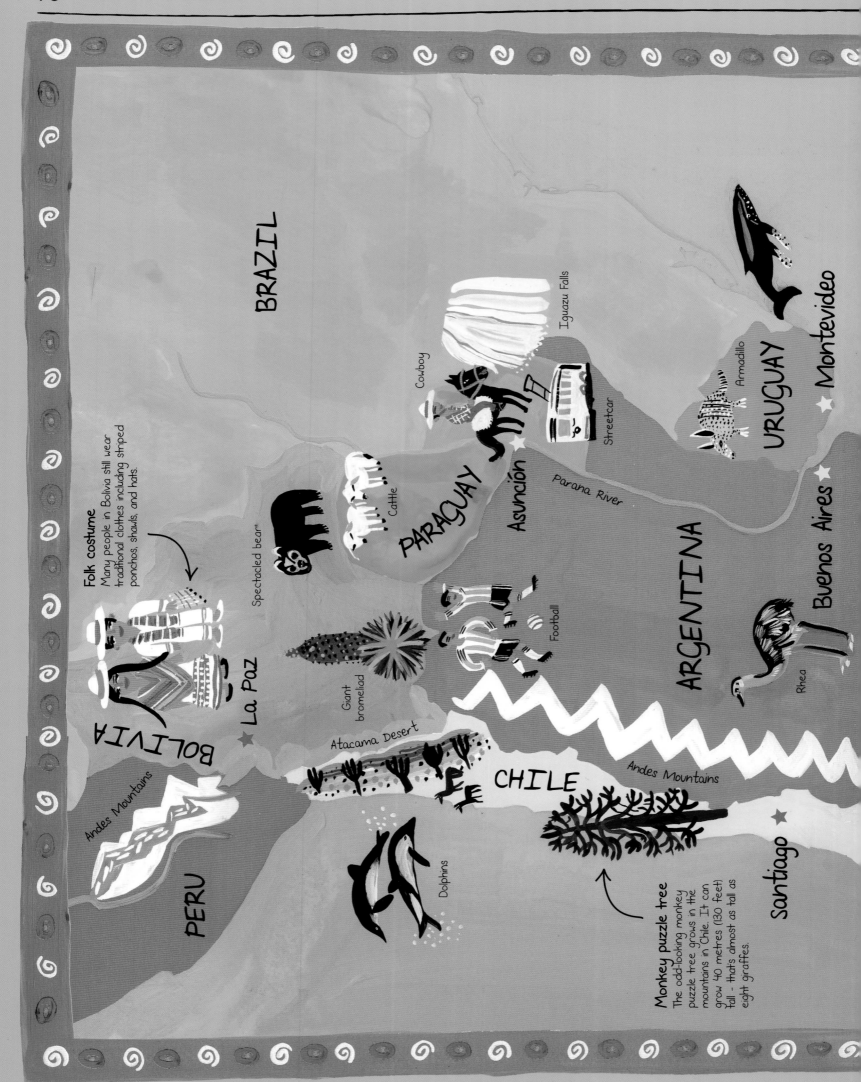

BRAZIL

PERU

BOLIVIA

Folk costume
Many people in Bolivia still wear traditional clothes including striped ponchos, shawls, and hats.

La Paz

Andes Mountains

Spectacled bear

Cattle

PARAGUAY

Cowboy

Iguazu Falls

Streetcar

Asunción

Parana River

URUGUAY

Montevideo

Armadillo

Giant bromeliad

Football

ARGENTINA

Buenos Aires

Rhea

Atacama Desert

CHILE

Andes Mountains

Santiago

Dolphins

Monkey puzzle tree
The odd-looking monkey puzzle tree grows in the mountains in Chile. It can grow 40 metres (130 feet) tall – that's almost as tall as eight giraffes.

Southern South America

Where do monkey puzzle trees grow?

The southern part of South America has a very varied landscape. Chile is a long, thin country that stretches along the west coast in between the sea and the Andes mountains. The Atacama Desert, in the north, is the driest place on Earth.

The pampas in Argentina and Uruguay are huge grassy plains used for growing crops and grazing cattle. At the southern tip of the region are the islands of Tierra del Fuego. They are wild and windswept with gigantic glaciers flowing from the mountains into the sea.

Tango dancers
The tango is a dramatic dance that began in Argentina and is now danced around the world. It is danced to music that can be happy or sad in mood.

Atlantic Ocean

Penguins

Falkland Islands

Pacific Ocean

Volcano

Grapes

Guanaco

Perito Moreno Glacier

Tierra del Fuego

Seals

Uruguay

Paraguay

Chile

Bolivia

Argentina

Europe

Europe is the world's second smallest continent – only Australia is smaller. Even so, around 750 million people live in Europe. Only Asia and Africa have more people. Europe is made up of many different countries, each with its own culture and, usually, its own language. The biggest country in Europe is Russia. Europe's smallest country is Vatican City in Italy.

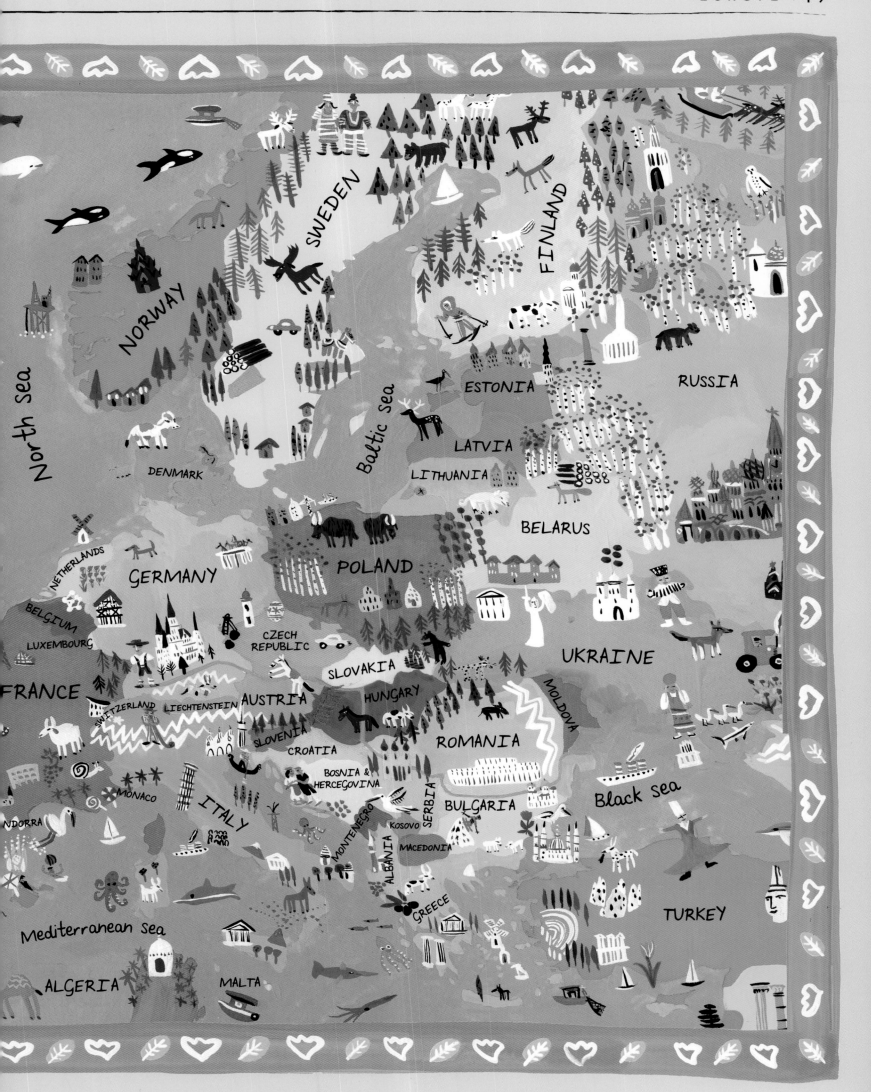

Shetland pony

Shetland Islands

Golf

Atlantic Ocean

Oil tanker

Loch Ness monster

Highland cow

Bagpipes
The bagpipes are a musical instrument played in Scotland. This player is wearing a kilt, a traditional Scottish garment made from tartan fabric.

Edinburgh

SCOTLAND

Hadrian's Wall

Cricket

North Sea

Leprechaun
Popular in Irish legends, leprechauns are types of fairies who like making mischief. They are usually shown as old men, about as tall as children.

NORTHERN IRELAND

Belfast

IRELAND

Red squirrel

Dublin

WALES

ENGLAND

Irish harp

Red dragon

London Eye

Big Ben

Blarney Castle

Corgi

Cardiff

London

Kingfisher

Stonehenge
Stonehenge is an ancient circle of stones. It was built more than 4,000 years ago and may have been a temple or burial site.

English Channel

British Isles

The British Isles is made up of the United Kingdom (Scotland, England, Wales and Northern Ireland) and Ireland. Most people in the British Isles speak English as their main language. The British Isles are famous for their history and traditions. Each year, millions of tourists visit the British Isles to see the sights. These include Buckingham Palace in London, England, the home of Queen Elizabeth II.

Ireland is a separate country to the United Kingdom. It has beautiful countryside and a mild but rainy climate. Its rich, green fields are used for grazing cattle.

Can you find someone playing golf?

United Kingdom

Ireland

Spain and Portugal

Can you find some golden sunflowers?

Spain

Portugal

Spain and Portugal lie in the south-west corner of Europe on a piece of land that juts out into the sea. The Pyrenees mountains in the north divide these two countries from the rest of Europe. The southern tip of Spain is only a few kilometres from Africa.

Spain and Portugal have sunny climates, sandy beaches and flavourful food. This makes them popular spots for holiday makers. Spain is also famous for its colourful fiestas (street festivals), and flamenco dancing. In Portugal, fishing along the Atlantic coast is an important industry, and people eat lots of fish and seafood here.

Atlantic Ocean

Guggenheim museum

FRANCE

ANDORRA

Pyrenees

Park Guell

Altamira cave paintings

PORTUGAL

Bullfighting
Bullfighting is a traditional sport in Spain. The matador tries to kill the bull with a spear. In some places, bullfighting has been banned because it is cruel.

Sunflowers

Barcelona

Madrid

Tomato fight

Majorca

Cork tree

Lisbon

SPAIN

Oranges

Flamenco dancer
Flamenco is a lively dance with lots of stamping and whirling around. Dancers click castanets, and are accompanied on the guitar.

Spanish lynx

Mediterranean Sea

Age of Discovery
In the 15th and 16th centuries, Portuguese and Spanish explorers set sail to find new trade routes around the world.

ALGERIA

MOROCCO

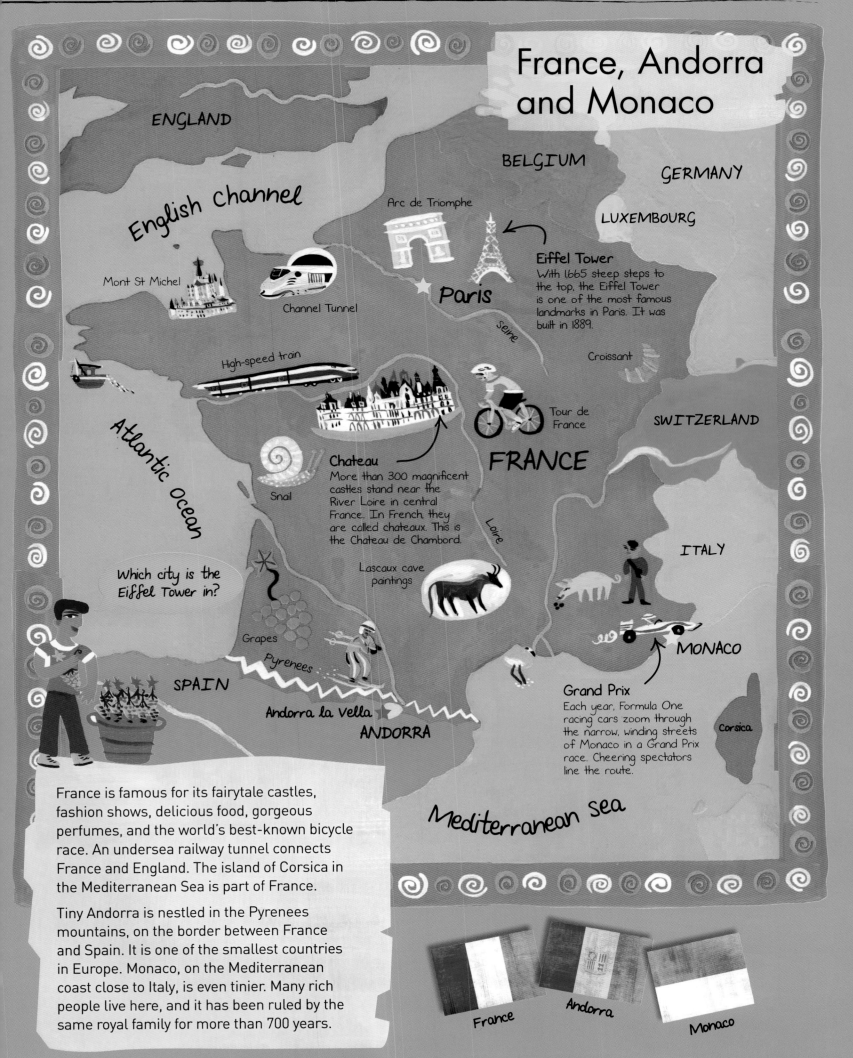

France, Andorra and Monaco

ENGLAND

English channel

BELGIUM

GERMANY

LUXEMBOURG

Arc de Triomphe

Eiffel Tower
With 1,665 steep steps to the top, the Eiffel Tower is one of the most famous landmarks in Paris. It was built in 1889.

Mont St Michel

Channel Tunnel

Paris

Seine

Croissant

High-speed train

Atlantic ocean

Snail

Chateau
More than 300 magnificent castles stand near the River Loire in central France. In French, they are called chateaux. This is the Chateau de Chambord.

Tour de France

FRANCE

Loire

SWITZERLAND

ITALY

Lascaux cave paintings

Which city is the Eiffel Tower in?

Grapes

Pyrenees

MONACO

Grand Prix
Each year, Formula One racing cars zoom through the narrow, winding streets of Monaco in a Grand Prix race. Cheering spectators line the route.

SPAIN

Andorra la Vella

ANDORRA

Corsica

Mediterranean sea

France is famous for its fairytale castles, fashion shows, delicious food, gorgeous perfumes, and the world's best-known bicycle race. An undersea railway tunnel connects France and England. The island of Corsica in the Mediterranean Sea is part of France.

Tiny Andorra is nestled in the Pyrenees mountains, on the border between France and Spain. It is one of the smallest countries in Europe. Monaco, on the Mediterranean coast close to Italy, is even tinier. Many rich people live here, and it has been ruled by the same royal family for more than 700 years.

France

Andorra

Monaco

Netherlands, Belgium and Luxembourg

North Sea

NETHERLANDS

Clogs

Wild boar

Tulips
Dutch farmers grow tulip bulbs and flowers to sell around the world. These lovely flowers come in many different colours.

Cheese market

Windmill
Windmills use wind power to pump water away from the land. They can also be used to grind grain to make flour.

Amsterdam ★

Bicycling

The Hague

Rhine River

Canal boats
The old city of Bruges in Belgium is criss-crossed by canals. Long, wide canal boats, called barges, carry goods and people around the city.

Delft pottery

Speed skating

Eurasian spoonbill

Red squirrel

Bruges

Mussels

Diamond

Antwerp

BELGIUM

GERMANY

Chocolates

Brussels ★

Mannekin Pis statue

Tintin and Snowy

Waffles

What is Tintin's dog called?

Handmade lace

Rollerskating

LUXEMBOURG

Ferris wheel

Red deer

★ Luxembourg

The Netherlands, Belgium and Luxembourg are known as the Low Countries because the land is so flat. Much of the Netherlands used to be underwater. People pumped away the water and turned the sea into farmland for growing crops. The flat land is also ideal for riding bicycles.

People speak Dutch in the Netherlands. In northern Belgium, people speak Flemish (a language similar to Dutch). In the south of Belgium, French is spoken. German, French and Luxembourgish are spoken in the tiny country of Luxembourg.

Netherlands

Belgium

Luxembourg

Answer: Snowy

Germany, Switzerland, Liechtenstein and Austria

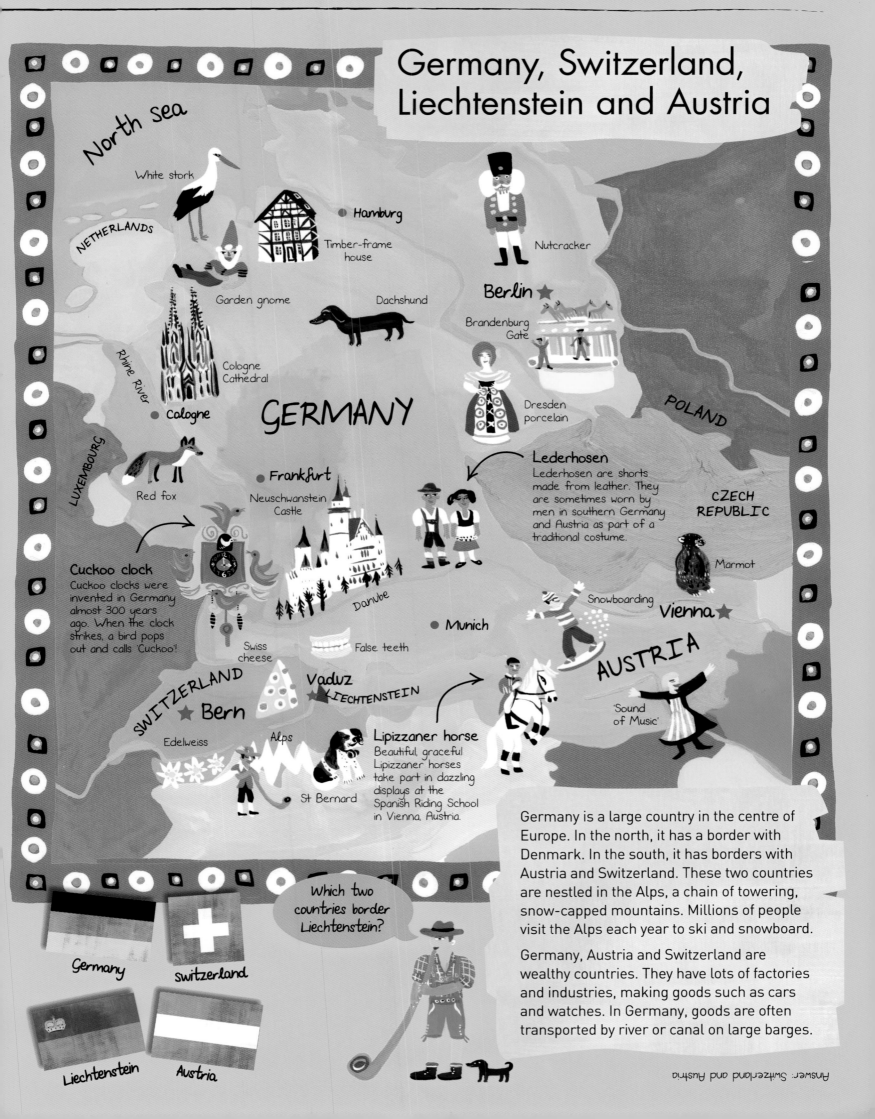

North Sea

White stork

NETHERLANDS

Timber-frame house

Hamburg

Nutcracker

Berlin

Brandenburg Gate

Garden gnome

Dachshund

Cologne Cathedral

Dresden porcelain

GERMANY

POLAND

Rhine River

Cologne

LUXEMBOURG

Red fox

Frankfurt

Neuschwanstein Castle

Lederhosen
Lederhosen are shorts made from leather. They are sometimes worn by men in southern Germany and Austria as part of a traditional costume.

CZECH REPUBLIC

Marmot

Cuckoo clock
Cuckoo clocks were invented in Germany almost 300 years ago. When the clock strikes, a bird pops out and calls 'Cuckoo'!

Danube

Snowboarding

Vienna

Munich

False teeth

AUSTRIA

Swiss cheese

Vaduz
LIECHTENSTEIN

SWITZERLAND
Bern

'Sound of Music'

Edelweiss

Alps

St Bernard

Lipizzaner horse
Beautiful, graceful Lipizzaner horses take part in dazzling displays at the Spanish Riding School in Vienna, Austria.

Germany is a large country in the centre of Europe. In the north, it has a border with Denmark. In the south, it has borders with Austria and Switzerland. These two countries are nestled in the Alps, a chain of towering, snow-capped mountains. Millions of people visit the Alps each year to ski and snowboard.

Germany, Austria and Switzerland are wealthy countries. They have lots of factories and industries, making goods such as cars and watches. In Germany, goods are often transported by river or canal on large barges.

Which two countries border Liechtenstein?

Germany

Switzerland

Liechtenstein

Austria

Answer: Switzerland and Austria

North Central Europe

Shipbuilding

Water festival

Horse-drawn sledge

Which country likes to put on puppet shows?

GERMANY

Astronomical clock

Prague

CZECH REPUBLIC

POLAND

Warsaw

Brown bear

Floating to Earth
Stefan Banic, from Slovakia, invented the parachute in 1914. To demonstrate how it worked, he bravely jumped from a 41st-storey window.

Czech puppet
Puppets are very popular in the Czech Republic. There are lots of theatres where you can watch puppet shows and shops that sell puppets.

Bratislava

SLOVAKIA

Turul bird

Budapest

HUNGARY

Count Dracula

Carpathian Mountains

Pelican

Csiko horseman
Csikos are cattle-herders from Hungary. They are skilful horse-riders, able to stand on two horses at the same time.

Rubik's cube

Dried peppers

Danube

ROMANIA

Gypsy cart

Bucharest

Black sea

Sofia

Bagpipes

BULGARIA

Martenitsa dolls

Roses

The countries of north central Europe are to the east of Germany and Austria. Most of this region is quite flat, but there are mountains in Slovakia. The great River Danube flows from Germany through Slovakia, Hungary and Romania before emptying into the Black Sea.

Some of Europe's most historical cities are found in this region. Prague is the capital of the Czech Republic. It is famous for its ancient buildings and bridges. Budapest is the capital of Hungary. It is actually two cities - Buda, on one bank of the River Danube, and Pest, on the other.

Poland   Czech Republic   Slovakia   Hungary   Romania   Bulgaria

Answer: Czech Republic

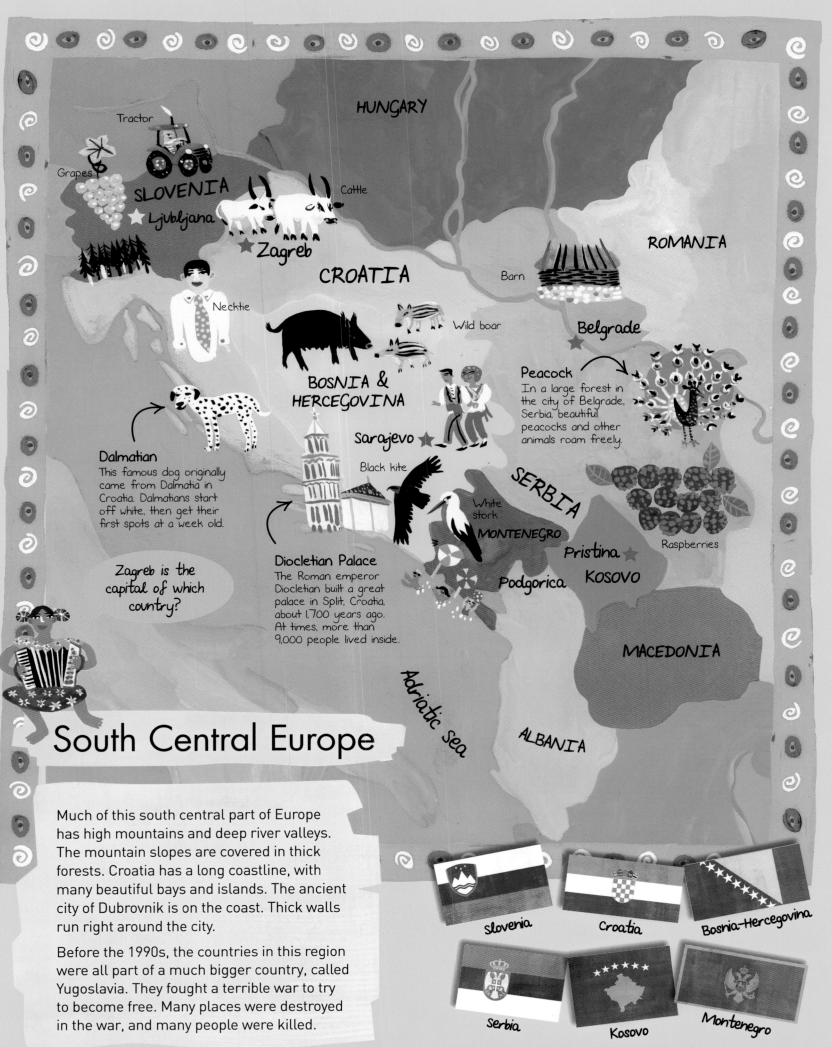

HUNGARY

Tractor

Grapes

SLOVENIA

Ljubljana

Cattle

Zagreb

CROATIA

Necktie

ROMANIA

Barn

Wild boar

Belgrade

Dalmatian
This famous dog originally came from Dalmatia in Croatia. Dalmatians start off white, then get their first spots at a week old.

BOSNIA & HERCEGOVINA

Sarajevo

Black kite

Peacock
In a large forest in the city of Belgrade, Serbia, beautiful peacocks and other animals roam freely.

SERBIA

White stork

MONTENEGRO

Raspberries

Pristina

Zagreb is the capital of which country?

Diocletian Palace
The Roman emperor Diocletian built a great palace in Split, Croatia, about 1,700 years ago. At times, more than 9,000 people lived inside.

Podgorica

KOSOVO

MACEDONIA

Adriatic sea

ALBANIA

South Central Europe

Much of this south central part of Europe has high mountains and deep river valleys. The mountain slopes are covered in thick forests. Croatia has a long coastline, with many beautiful bays and islands. The ancient city of Dubrovnik is on the coast. Thick walls run right around the city.

Before the 1990s, the countries in this region were all part of a much bigger country, called Yugoslavia. They fought a terrible war to try to become free. Many places were destroyed in the war, and many people were killed.

Slovenia

Croatia

Bosnia-Hercegovina

Serbia

Kosovo

Montenegro

Answer: Croatia

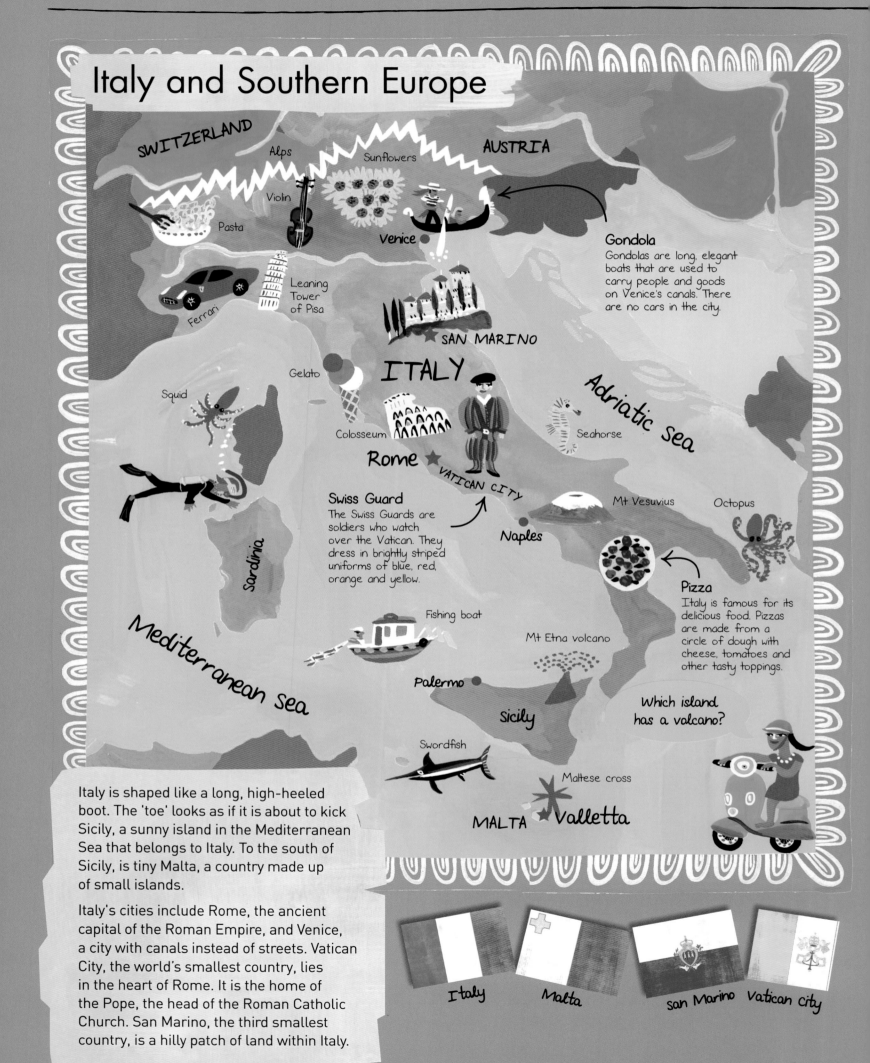

Italy and Southern Europe

SWITZERLAND

Alps

Sunflowers

AUSTRIA

Violin

Pasta

Ferrari

Leaning Tower of Pisa

Venice

Gondola
Gondolas are long, elegant boats that are used to carry people and goods on Venice's canals. There are no cars in the city.

SAN MARINO

Gelato

ITALY

Squid

Colosseum

Rome

VATICAN CITY

Swiss Guard
The Swiss Guards are soldiers who watch over the Vatican. They dress in brightly striped uniforms of blue, red, orange and yellow.

Sardinia

Mediterranean Sea

Fishing boat

Naples

Mt Vesuvius

Seahorse

Adriatic Sea

Octopus

Pizza
Italy is famous for its delicious food. Pizzas are made from a circle of dough with cheese, tomatoes and other tasty toppings.

Mt Etna volcano

Palermo

Sicily

Which island has a volcano?

Swordfish

Maltese cross

MALTA   Valletta

Italy is shaped like a long, high-heeled boot. The 'toe' looks as if it is about to kick Sicily, a sunny island in the Mediterranean Sea that belongs to Italy. To the south of Sicily, is tiny Malta, a country made up of small islands.

Italy's cities include Rome, the ancient capital of the Roman Empire, and Venice, a city with canals instead of streets. Vatican City, the world's smallest country, lies in the heart of Rome. It is the home of the Pope, the head of the Roman Catholic Church. San Marino, the third smallest country, is a hilly patch of land within Italy.

Italy   Malta   San Marino   Vatican city

Answer: Sicily

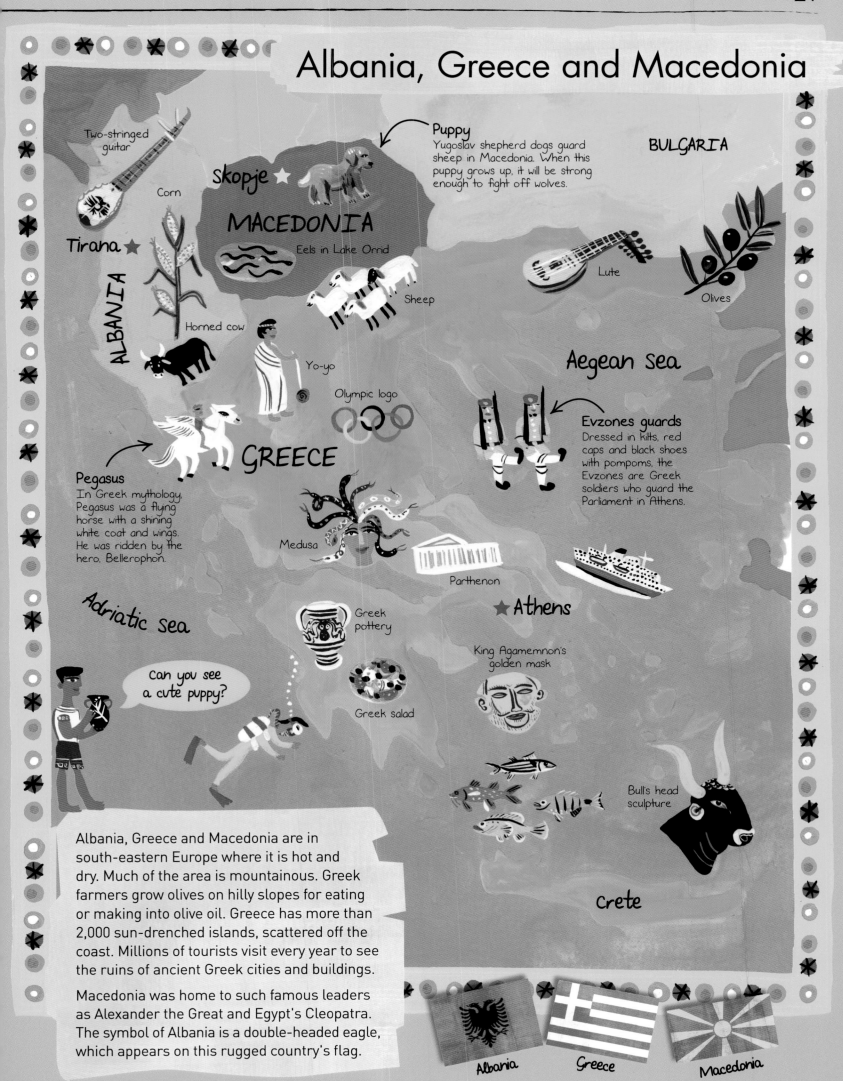

Albania, Greece and Macedonia

Two-stringed guitar

Skopje

Corn

MACEDONIA

Tirana

ALBANIA

Eels in Lake Ohrid

Puppy
Yugoslav shepherd dogs guard sheep in Macedonia. When this puppy grows up, it will be strong enough to fight off wolves.

BULGARIA

Lute

Olives

Horned cow

Sheep

Yo-yo

Aegean sea

Olympic logo

GREECE

Pegasus
In Greek mythology, Pegasus was a flying horse with a shining white coat and wings. He was ridden by the hero, Bellerophon.

Evzones guards
Dressed in kilts, red caps and black shoes with pompoms, the Evzones are Greek soldiers who guard the Parliament in Athens.

Medusa

Parthenon

Adriatic sea

Greek pottery

Can you see a cute puppy?

Greek salad

Athens

King Agamemnon's golden mask

Bull's head sculpture

Crete

Albania, Greece and Macedonia are in south-eastern Europe where it is hot and dry. Much of the area is mountainous. Greek farmers grow olives on hilly slopes for eating or making into olive oil. Greece has more than 2,000 sun-drenched islands, scattered off the coast. Millions of tourists visit every year to see the ruins of ancient Greek cities and buildings.

Macedonia was home to such famous leaders as Alexander the Great and Egypt's Cleopatra. The symbol of Albania is a double-headed eagle, which appears on this rugged country's flag.

Albania

Greece

Macedonia

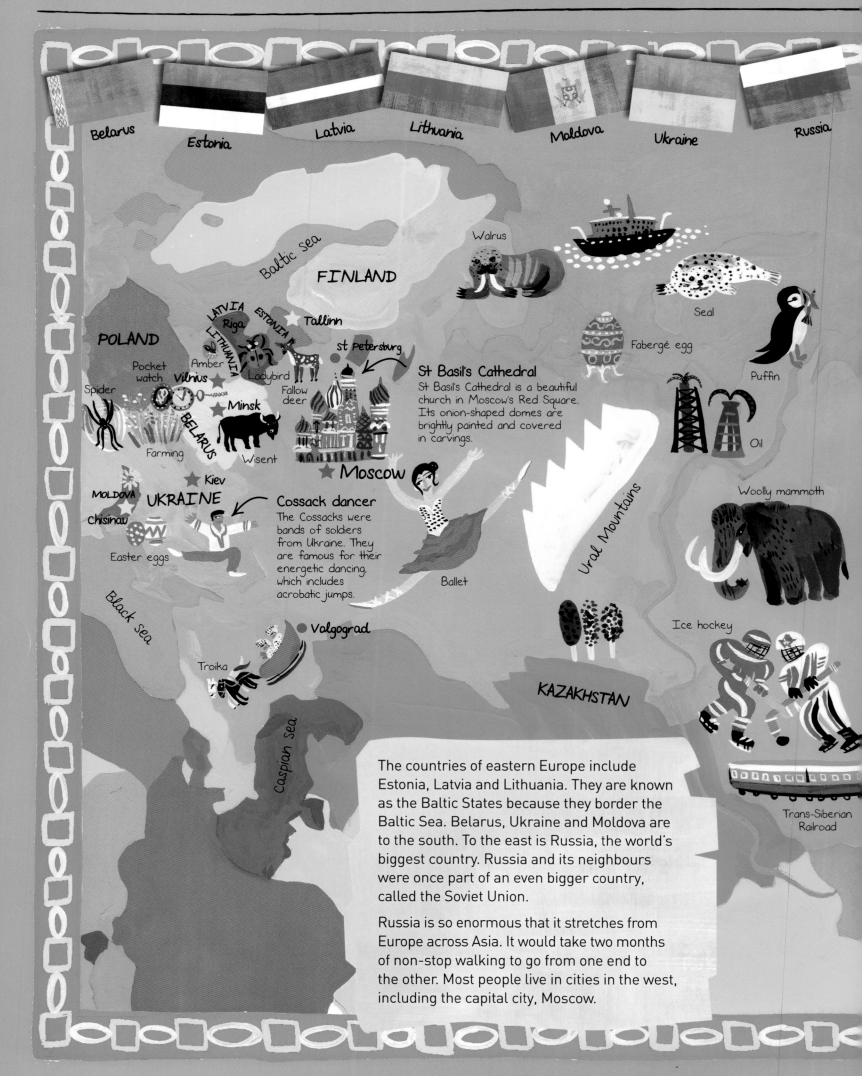

Belarus
Estonia
Latvia
Lithuania
Moldova
Ukraine
Russia

Baltic Sea

FINLAND

Walrus

Seal

Fabergé egg

Puffin

POLAND

LATVIA
Riga
ESTONIA
Tallinn

LITHUANIA

st Petersburg

Pocket watch
Amber
Vilnius
Ladybird

Fallow deer

St Basil's Cathedral

St Basil's Cathedral is a beautiful church in Moscow's Red Square. Its onion-shaped domes are brightly painted and covered in carvings.

Oil

Spider

Minsk

BELARUS

Wisent

Farming

Moscow

Woolly mammoth

MOLDOVA
Kiev

UKRAINE

Chisinau

Easter eggs

Cossack dancer

The Cossacks were bands of soldiers from Ukraine. They are famous for their energetic dancing, which includes acrobatic jumps.

Ballet

Ural Mountains

Ice hockey

Black Sea

Volgograd

Troika

KAZAKHSTAN

Caspian Sea

Trans-Siberian Railroad

The countries of eastern Europe include Estonia, Latvia and Lithuania. They are known as the Baltic States because they border the Baltic Sea. Belarus, Ukraine and Moldova are to the south. To the east is Russia, the world's biggest country. Russia and its neighbours were once part of an even bigger country, called the Soviet Union.

Russia is so enormous that it stretches from Europe across Asia. It would take two months of non-stop walking to go from one end to the other. Most people live in cities in the west, including the capital city, Moscow.

Baltic States and Russia

Matryoshka doll
Russian matryoshka dolls are a set of wooden dolls that get smaller and smaller. They are placed inside each other, in order of size.

Arctic Ocean

Polar bears

Arctic fox

Yakut inuit

Wolf

RUSSIA

Chess

Oil
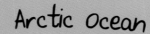

Volcano

Horseback riding

Kamchatka Peninsula

Gymnastics

Reindeer sledge

Salmon

Siberian house

Siberian tiger

Irkutsk

Lake Baikal

Pacific Ocean

Which mountains are in Russia?

MONGOLIA

Vladivostok

Asia

Asia is truly enormous – the largest continent on Earth. Covering almost a third of Earth's land area, it stretches from the Arctic in the north to the Equator in the south, and from the Mediterranean Sea in the west to the Pacific Ocean in the east. Asia has 48 countries and is home to more than 3.8 billion people – about two out of every three of us on the planet.

RUSSIA

MONGOLIA

KYRGYZSTAN

TAJIKISTAN

CHINA

NORTH
KOREA

SOUTH
KOREA

JAPAN

TIBET

NEPAL

BHUTAN

BANGLADESH

INDIA

MYANMAR

TAIWAN

LAOS

THAILAND

VIETNAM

CAMBODIA

PHILIPPINES

Pacific Ocean

SRI
LANKA

MALDIVES

BRUNEI

MALAYSIA

SINGAPORE

INDONESIA

EAST TIMOR

PAPUA
NEW
GUINEA

Indian Ocean

AUSTRALIA

Middle East

RUSSIA

Whirling dervish
Dervishes are religious followers from Turkey. As part of their worship, they perform spectacular dances, spinning round and round and round.

Black sea

Caspian sea

Folk costumes

GEORGIA ★ Tbilisi

Anchovies

Copper pot   ARMENIA AZERBAIJAN   Baku

Yerevan

Blue Mosque

Ankara ★

TURKEY

Turkish rug

Goats

Coffee

Temple of the Fire Worshippers

Turkish delight
Turkish delight is a jelly-like sweet. It can be mixed with chopped nuts and flavourings like rose water. It is cut into small cubes and dusted with icing sugar.

Amphitheatre at Palmyra

Lemons

Nicosia
CYPRUS ★

Cedar

SYRIA

Date palms

Tigris

Mediterranean sea

Olives

Beirut LEBANON
        ★ Damascus

Lamb

Euphrates

IRAQ

Jerusalem

PALESTINE

Amman   Petra

ISRAEL

Dome of the Rock

JORDAN

Dome of the Rock
The Dome of the Rock in Jerusalem is a holy place for Muslims. They believe the Prophet Muhammad left from here on a visit to heaven.

EGYPT

Red sea

Which country has a tree on its flag?

SAUDI ARABIA

The part of Asia closest to Europe is called the Middle East. In the past, this region was an important crossroads for trade between three continents – Europe, Asia and Africa. Turkey is the largest country in the region. It lies mostly in Asia with a small part in Europe. Its biggest city, Istanbul, is the only city in the world that sits in two continents.

Many people in the Middle East are Muslims. They follow the religion of Islam. Two other great religions – Judaism and Christianity – also began in the region.

Turkey

Georgia

Cyprus

Armenia

Azerbaijan

Syria

Lebanon

Israel

Jordan

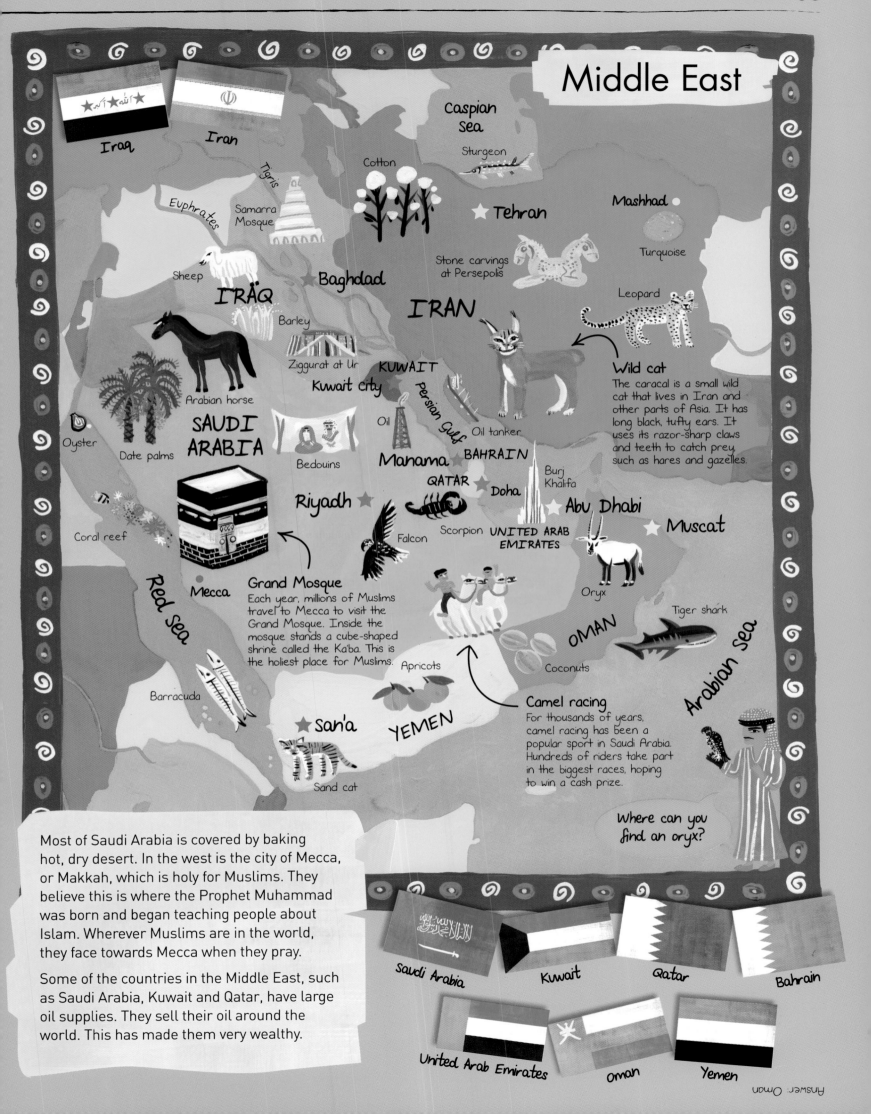

Middle East

Iraq

Iran

Caspian Sea

Cotton

Sturgeon

Mashhad

Tehran

Turquoise

Tigris

Euphrates

Samarra Mosque

Leopard

Sheep

Baghdad

IRAN

IRAQ

Barley

Stone carvings at Persepolis

Wild cat

The caracal is a small wild cat that lives in Iran and other parts of Asia. It has long black, tufty ears. It uses its razor-sharp claws and teeth to catch prey, such as hares and gazelles.

Ziggurat at Ur

KUWAIT

Kuwait city

Persian Gulf

Oil tanker

Arabian horse

SAUDI ARABIA

Oil

Oyster

Date palms

Bedouins

Mahama

BAHRAIN

Burj Khalifa

QATAR

Doha

Abu Dhabi

Muscat

Riyadh

Scorpion

UNITED ARAB EMIRATES

Coral reef

Falcon

Oryx

Tiger shark

Grand Mosque

Each year, millions of Muslims travel to Mecca to visit the Grand Mosque. Inside the mosque stands a cube-shaped shrine called the Ka'ba. This is the holiest place for Muslims.

Mecca

Red sea

OMAN

Coconuts

Apricots

Camel racing

For thousands of years, camel racing has been a popular sport in Saudi Arabia. Hundreds of riders take part in the biggest races, hoping to win a cash prize.

Barracuda

San'a

YEMEN

Arabian Sea

Sand cat

Where can you find an oryx?

Most of Saudi Arabia is covered by baking hot, dry desert. In the west is the city of Mecca, or Makkah, which is holy for Muslims. They believe this is where the Prophet Muhammad was born and began teaching people about Islam. Wherever Muslims are in the world, they face towards Mecca when they pray.

Some of the countries in the Middle East, such as Saudi Arabia, Kuwait and Qatar, have large oil supplies. They sell their oil around the world. This has made them very wealthy.

Saudi Arabia

Kuwait

Qatar

Bahrain

United Arab Emirates

Oman

Yemen

Answer: Oman

Kazakhstan

Kyrgyzstan

Tajikistan

Turkmenistan

Uzbekistan

RUSSIA

Traditional tent
Many people in Central Asia traditionally lived as nomads. They moved from place to place with their animals. They lived in tents, called yurts, that were quick and easy to put up and take down.

Marmot

Apple trees

Riders on horseback

Aral sea

Boat stranded in sand near Aral sea

Bowl of caviar

Folk costume

Caspian sea

UZBEKISTAN

TURKMENISTAN

Mausoleum in Samarkand

Colourful rug

Brown horse

Cotton plant

Ashgabat

Sheep

IRAN

AFGHANISTAN

Central Asia

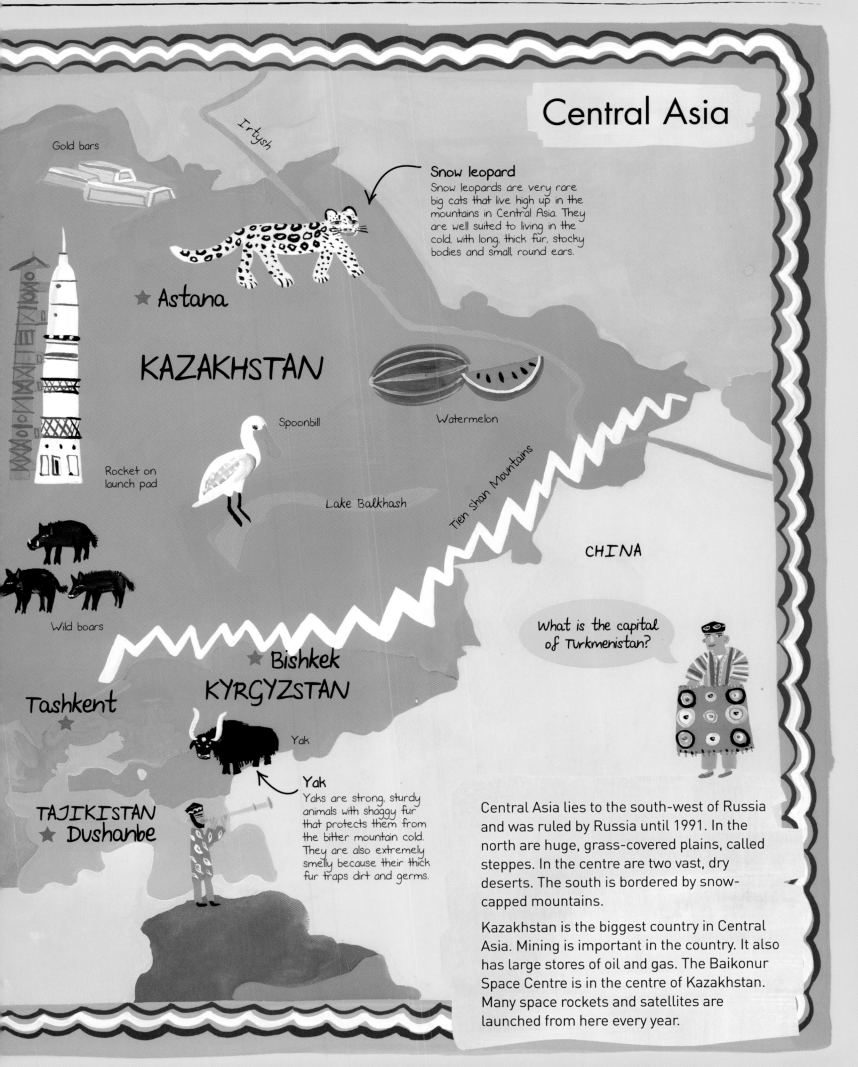

Gold bars

Irtysh

Snow leopard
Snow leopards are very rare big cats that live high up in the mountains in Central Asia. They are well suited to living in the cold, with long, thick fur, stocky bodies and small, round ears.

★ Astana

KAZAKHSTAN

Spoonbill

Watermelon

Rocket on launch pad

Lake Balkhash

Tien Shan Mountains

CHINA

Wild boars

What is the capital of Turkmenistan?

★ Bishkek
KYRGYZSTAN

Tashkent

Yak

Yak
Yaks are strong, sturdy animals with shaggy fur that protects them from the bitter mountain cold. They are also extremely smelly because their thick fur traps dirt and germs.

TAJIKISTAN
★ Dushanbe

Central Asia lies to the south-west of Russia and was ruled by Russia until 1991. In the north are huge, grass-covered plains, called steppes. In the centre are two vast, dry deserts. The south is bordered by snow-capped mountains.

Kazakhstan is the biggest country in Central Asia. Mining is important in the country. It also has large stores of oil and gas. The Baikonur Space Centre is in the centre of Kazakhstan. Many space rockets and satellites are launched from here every year.

Afghanistan and Pakistan

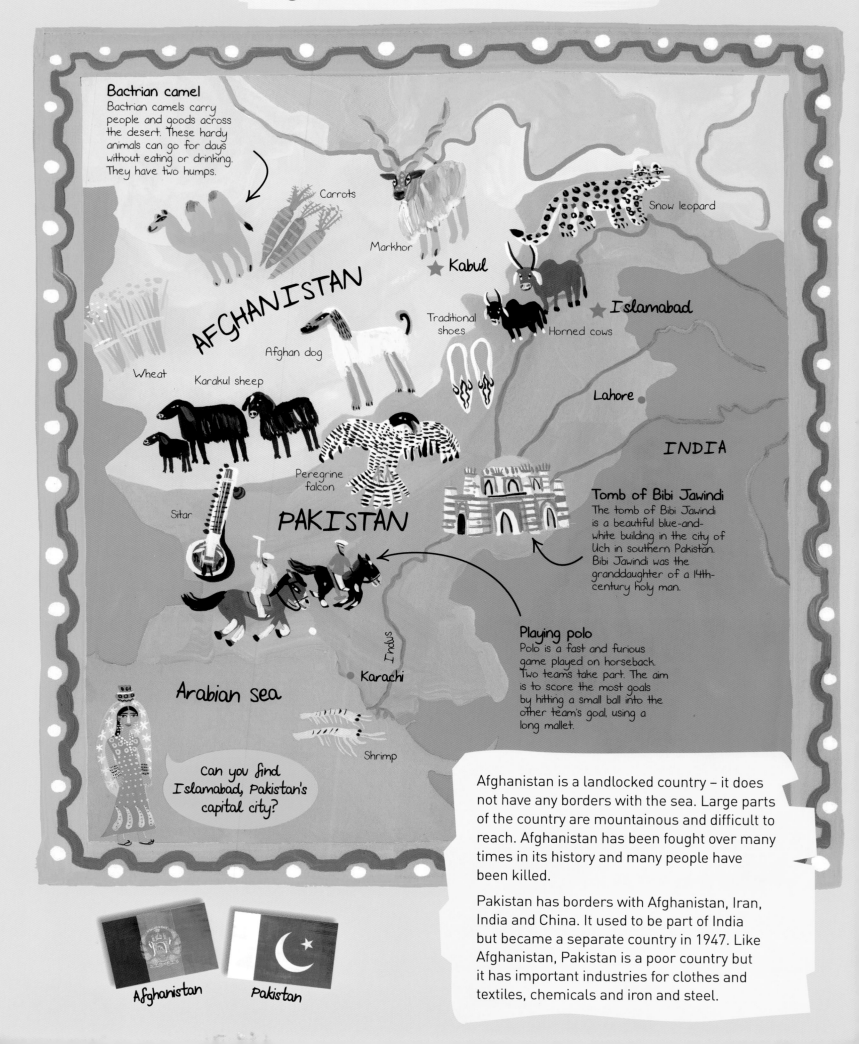

Bactrian camel
Bactrian camels carry people and goods across the desert. These hardy animals can go for days without eating or drinking. They have two humps.

Carrots

Markhor

Snow leopard

★ Kabul

AFGHANISTAN

Traditional shoes

★ Islamabad

Horned cows

Afghan dog

Wheat

Karakul sheep

Lahore

INDIA

Peregrine falcon

Tomb of Bibi Jawindi
The tomb of Bibi Jawindi is a beautiful blue-and-white building in the city of Uch in southern Pakistan. Bibi Jawindi was the granddaughter of a 14th-century holy man.

Sitar

PAKISTAN

Playing polo
Polo is a fast and furious game played on horseback. Two teams take part. The aim is to score the most goals by hitting a small ball into the other team's goal, using a long mallet.

Indus

Karachi

Arabian sea

Shrimp

Can you find Islamabad, Pakistan's capital city?

Afghanistan is a landlocked country – it does not have any borders with the sea. Large parts of the country are mountainous and difficult to reach. Afghanistan has been fought over many times in its history and many people have been killed.

Pakistan has borders with Afghanistan, Iran, India and China. It used to be part of India but became a separate country in 1947. Like Afghanistan, Pakistan is a poor country but it has important industries for clothes and textiles, chemicals and iron and steel.

Afghanistan

Pakistan

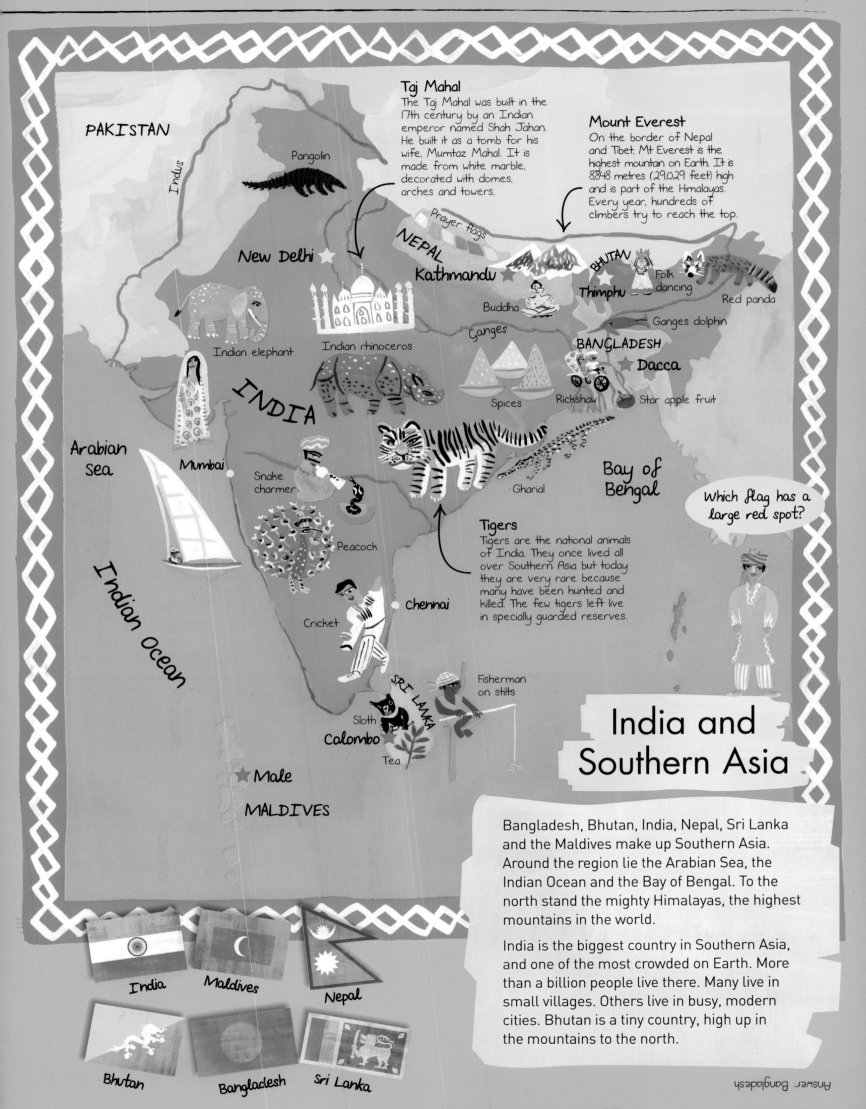

Taj Mahal

The Taj Mahal was built in the 17th century by an Indian emperor named Shah Jahan. He built it as a tomb for his wife, Mumtaz Mahal. It is made from white marble, decorated with domes, arches and towers.

Mount Everest

On the border of Nepal and Tibet, Mt Everest is the highest mountain on Earth. It is 8,848 metres (29,029 feet) high and is part of the Himalayas. Every year, hundreds of climbers try to reach the top.

PAKISTAN

Indus

Pangolin

New Delhi

Prayer flags

NEPAL

Kathmandu

BHUTAN

Thimphu

Folk dancing

Red panda

Buddha

Ganges

Ganges dolphin

BANGLADESH

Dacca

Indian elephant

Indian rhinoceros

INDIA

Arabian Sea

Mumbai

Spices

Rickshaw

Star apple fruit

Snake charmer

Gharial

Bay of Bengal

Which flag has a large red spot?

Peacock

Tigers

Tigers are the national animals of India. They once lived all over Southern Asia but today they are very rare because many have been hunted and killed. The few tigers left live in specially guarded reserves.

Indian Ocean

Cricket

Chennai

SRI LANKA

Fisherman on stilts

Sloth

Colombo

Tea

India and Southern Asia

Male

MALDIVES

Bangladesh, Bhutan, India, Nepal, Sri Lanka and the Maldives make up Southern Asia. Around the region lie the Arabian Sea, the Indian Ocean and the Bay of Bengal. To the north stand the mighty Himalayas, the highest mountains in the world.

India is the biggest country in Southern Asia, and one of the most crowded on Earth. More than a billion people live there. Many live in small villages. Others live in busy, modern cities. Bhutan is a tiny country, high up in the mountains to the north.

India   Maldives   Nepal

Bhutan   Bangladesh   Sri Lanka

Answer: Bangladesh

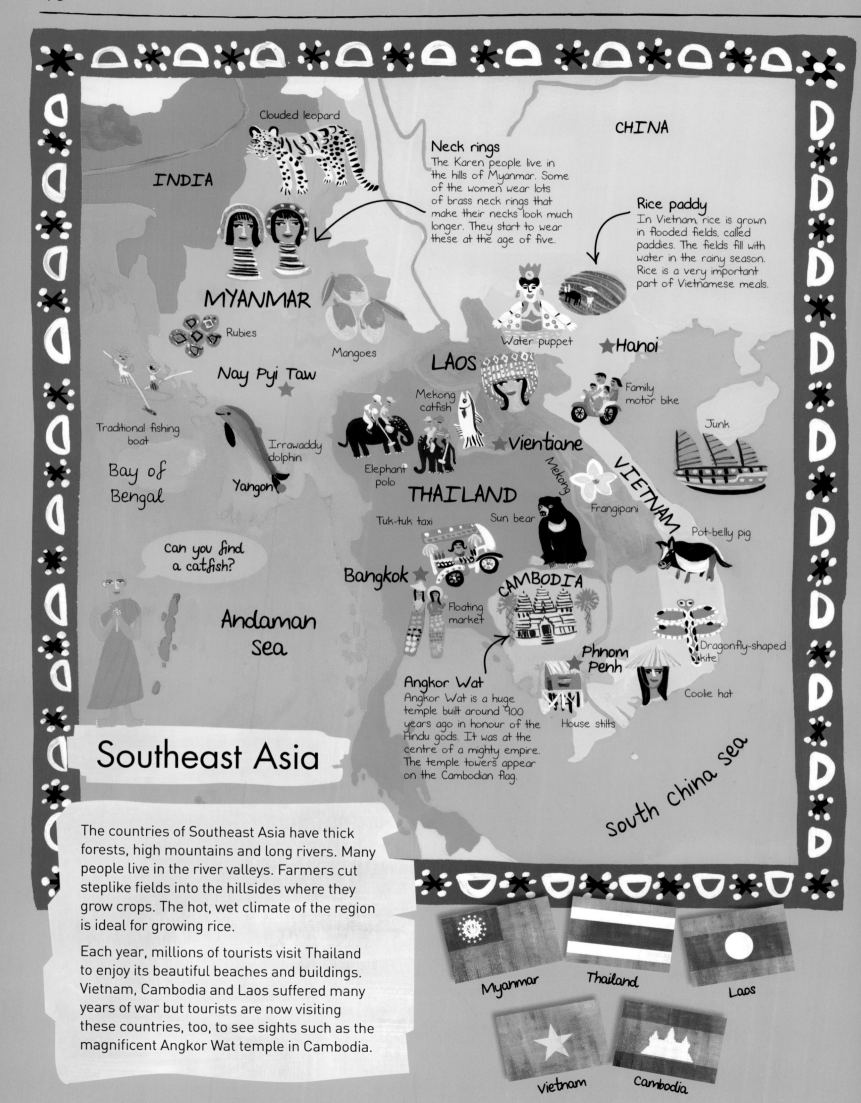

Clouded leopard

CHINA

INDIA

Neck rings
The Karen people live in the hills of Myanmar. Some of the women wear lots of brass neck rings that make their necks look much longer. They start to wear these at the age of five.

Rice paddy
In Vietnam, rice is grown in flooded fields, called paddies. The fields fill with water in the rainy season. Rice is a very important part of Vietnamese meals.

MYANMAR

Rubies

Mangoes

Water puppet

Hanoi

LAOS

Nay Pyi Taw

Mekong catfish

Family motor bike

Junk

Traditional fishing boat

Irrawaddy dolphin

Elephant polo

Vientiane

VIETNAM

Bay of Bengal

Yangon

THAILAND

Mekong

Frangipani

Sun bear

Pot-belly pig

can you find a catfish?

Tuk-tuk taxi

Bangkok

CAMBODIA

Dragonfly-shaped kite

Andaman Sea

Floating market

Phnom Penh

Coolie hat

Angkor Wat
Angkor Wat is a huge temple built around 900 years ago in honour of the Hindu gods. It was at the centre of a mighty empire. The temple towers appear on the Cambodian flag.

House stilts

Southeast Asia

South China Sea

The countries of Southeast Asia have thick forests, high mountains and long rivers. Many people live in the river valleys. Farmers cut steplike fields into the hillsides where they grow crops. The hot, wet climate of the region is ideal for growing rice.

Each year, millions of tourists visit Thailand to enjoy its beautiful beaches and buildings. Vietnam, Cambodia and Laos suffered many years of war but tourists are now visiting these countries, too, to see sights such as the magnificent Angkor Wat temple in Cambodia.

Myanmar

Thailand

Laos

Vietnam

Cambodia

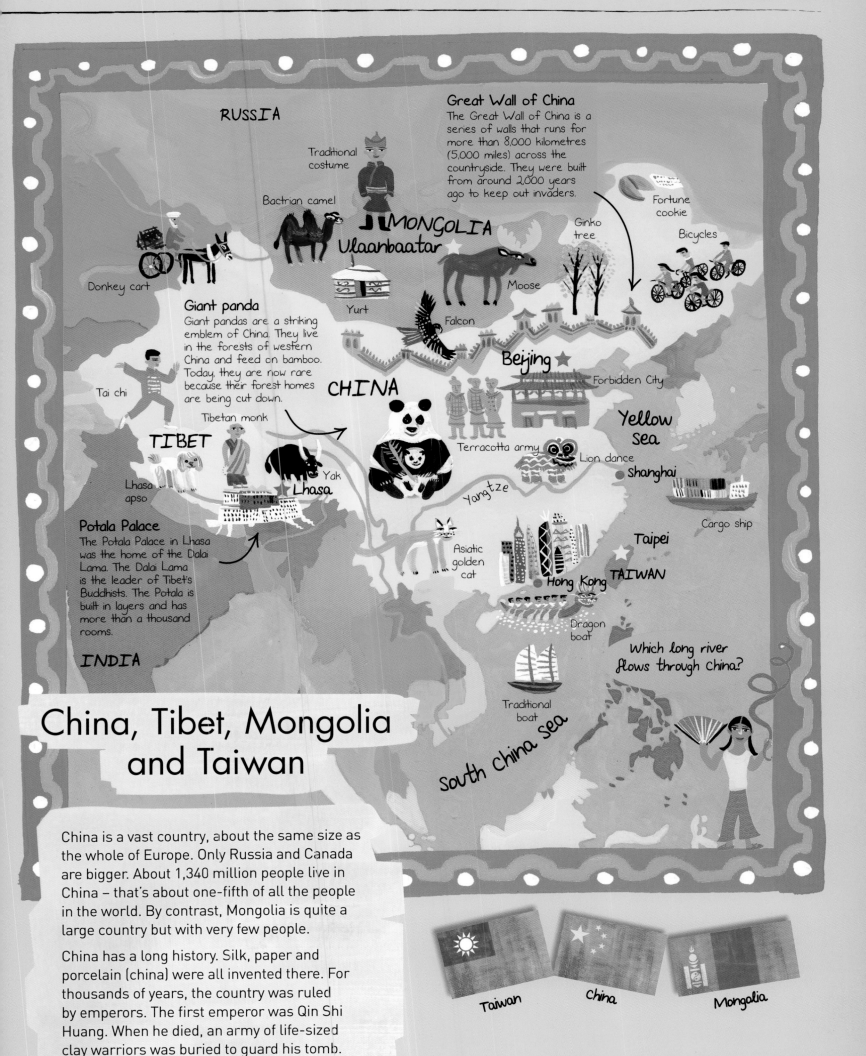

RUSSIA

Traditional costume

Bactrian camel

MONGOLIA
Ulaanbaatar

Yurt

Moose

Falcon

Donkey cart

Giant panda
Giant pandas are a striking emblem of China. They live in the forests of western China and feed on bamboo. Today, they are now rare because their forest homes are being cut down.

Tai chi

Tibetan monk

TIBET

Lhasa apso

Yak

Lhasa

CHINA

Terracotta army

Lion dance

Great Wall of China
The Great Wall of China is a series of walls that runs for more than 8,000 kilometres (5,000 miles) across the countryside. They were built from around 2,000 years ago to keep out invaders.

Ginko tree

Fortune cookie

Bicycles

Beijing

Forbidden City

Yellow Sea

Shanghai

Cargo ship

Potala Palace
The Potala Palace in Lhasa was the home of the Dalai Lama. The Dalai Lama is the leader of Tibet's Buddhists. The Potala is built in layers and has more than a thousand rooms.

INDIA

Yangtze

Asiatic golden cat

Hong Kong

Taipei

TAIWAN

Dragon boat

Which long river flows through China?

Traditional boat

South China Sea

China, Tibet, Mongolia and Taiwan

China is a vast country, about the same size as the whole of Europe. Only Russia and Canada are bigger. About 1,340 million people live in China – that's about one-fifth of all the people in the world. By contrast, Mongolia is quite a large country but with very few people.

China has a long history. Silk, paper and porcelain (china) were all invented there. For thousands of years, the country was ruled by emperors. The first emperor was Qin Shi Huang. When he died, an army of life-sized clay warriors was buried to guard his tomb.

Taiwan

China

Mongolia

North and South Korea

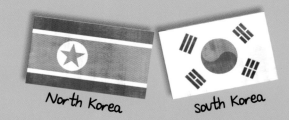

North Korea

South Korea

The Korean Peninsula is a piece of land in Asia that juts out into the Pacific Ocean. It is split into two countries – North Korea and South Korea. Both have high mountains and thick forests. In winter, the weather is bitterly cold. In summer, it can be very hot and sticky.

North Korea has a strict government that does not allow much contact with the outside world. South Korea is much more open. It trades with many other countries, including Japan and the USA, selling products such as computers, cars and electronic goods.

Traditional costume

Chollima

Cargo ship

Magnolia blossom

Sino-Korean Friendship Bridge

CHINA

NORTH KOREA

'Dear Leader' statue

P'yongyang

Farmer carrying grain

Gymnastics
Gymnastics are popular in North Korea. On national holidays, tens of thousands of gymnasts take part in huge displays. Young gymnasts spend months and years in training.

Smelting iron

Gyeongbokgung Palace

Ice sculpture
Every winter, ice festivals are held in cities around North Korea. The festivals feature spectacular ice sculptures that take many months to make.

Seoul

SOUTH KOREA

Octopus

Stone sculpture

Hibiscus flower

Hyundai car

Fan dancers
Women dancers in South Korea perform spectacular fan dances. As they dance, they move faster and faster, making patterns of flowers, butterflies and waves with their fans.

Swordfish

KTX high-speed train

Pusan

Squid

JAPAN

Can you see a hibiscus flower?

Tae kwon do

Yellow Sea

Sea of Japan

CHINA

RUSSIA

NORTH KOREA

SOUTH KOREA

Sea of Japan

Skier

Macaque

Hokkaido

Mako shark

Japanese crane

Origami

Sushi
Sushi is a famous Japanese dish. It is made up of small pieces of raw fish, seaweed and rice. Japanese people eat more fish and seafood than anyone else in the world.

Origami
Origami means 'paper folding' and is a traditional Japanese art. Experts can make complicated models of animals, objects and shapes out of simple sheets of paper.

Kabuki theatre

Puffer fish

Sumo wrestler
Sumo is Japanese wrestling. Wrestlers are very heavy and have to train hard at special Sumo schools. They try to throw each other out of a circular ring, called a dohyo.

Himeji Castle

Manga

Woman wearing kimono

JAPAN   Honshu

Pagoda

Tokyo

Mt Fuji

Osaka

Torii Gate

Cherry blossom

Pearl diver

Traditional fishing boat

Pacific Ocean

Philippine Sea

What is the capital of Japan?

Japan

Japan is a chain of thousands of islands in East Asia. Most people live on the four biggest islands - Hokkaido, Honshu, Shikoku and Kyushu. The countryside is hilly with not much land left for farming and building on, so many people live in cities by the coast. The capital city is Tokyo, one of the busiest and biggest cities in the world.

Japan is a modern, wealthy country but traditions are still very important. At special times, people wear traditional, long-sleeved robes called kimonos, and wooden sandals.

Japan

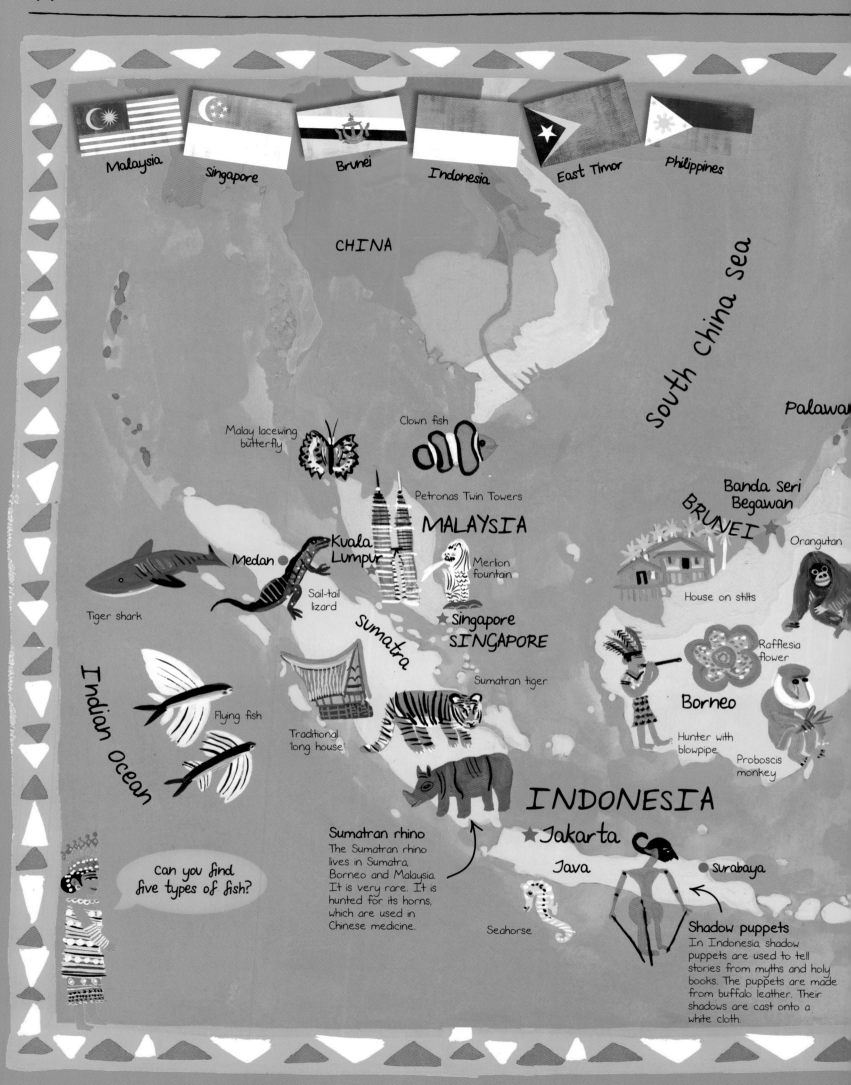

Malaysia

Singapore

Brunei

Indonesia

East Timor

Philippines

CHINA

South China Sea

Palawan

Malay lacewing butterfly

Clown fish

Petronas Twin Towers

MALAYSIA

Kuala Lumpur

Medan

Sail-tail lizard

Tiger shark

Indian Ocean

Sumatra

Merlion fountain

Singapore
SINGAPORE

Banda Seri Begawan

BRUNEI

Orangutan

House on stilts

Rafflesia flower

Borneo

Hunter with blowpipe

Proboscis monkey

Sumatran tiger

Flying fish

Traditional 'long house'

INDONESIA

Jakarta

Java

Surabaya

Sumatran rhino
The Sumatran rhino lives in Sumatra, Borneo and Malaysia. It is very rare. It is hunted for its horns, which are used in Chinese medicine.

Can you find five types of fish?

Seahorse

Shadow puppets
In Indonesia, shadow puppets are used to tell stories from myths and holy books. The puppets are made from buffalo leather. Their shadows are cast onto a white cloth.

Eastern Seas

Off the coast of mainland Southeast Asia lie thousands of islands, stretching out towards the Pacific Ocean. Many are covered in hot, steamy rainforests and active volcanoes. The country of Singapore is a tiny island off the tip of Malaysia. At the other end of the scale, Indonesia is a country made up of more than 13,000 islands.

The islands are home to some extraordinary animals. Among them is the Komodo dragon, the world's biggest lizard. It is found only on a few islands in Indonesia.

Swordfish

Luzon

Jeepney

Traditional fishing boat

Manila

Parrotfish

PHILIPPINES

Coconuts

Stick dancing

Tinikling is a traditional stick dance from the Philippines. One person taps two sticks together on the ground while others dance over and between them. The dancers have to be quick on their feet.

Mindanao

Davao

Philippine eagle

Coral reef

Batik cloth

Sulawesi

Tarsier

Pacific Ocean

Scuba diver

Corn

Dili

EAST TIMOR

Hammerhead shark

Komodo dragon

Manta ray

New Guinea

Bananas

Greater bird of paradise

AUSTRALIA

Oceania

Oceania is made up of Australia – the world's smallest continent – New Zealand, Papua New Guinea and hundreds of tiny islands that are scattered over a huge area of the Pacific Ocean. The region has many different types of landscapes, from tropical rainforests and coral reefs, to volcanoes and glaciers. Some 35 million people live in Oceania.

PALAU

AUSTRALIA

Pacific Ocean

Indian Ocean

Leafy
seadragon

Aboriginal man
playing didgeridoo

Crocodile

Giant termite
mound

Great Barrier Reef
The Great Barrier Reef
is the world's largest coral
reef. It stretches for
more than 2,600 kilometres
(1,600 miles) and is home to
a huge number of creatures,
including more than 1,500
species of fish.

Uluru
Uluru (Ayers Rock) is a
massive block of sandstone
about 350 metres (1,150
feet) tall. It is a sacred
place for the Aboriginal
people. Caves at the base
of the rock are decorated
with ancient paintings.

Oyster
with pearl

Boomerang

Rock paintings

Emu

Tropical
rainforest

Echidna

Brown snake

AUSTRALIA

Dingo

Koala

Brisbane

Grey kangaroo

Sydney
Opera House

Herding sheep

Opals

Red kangaroo
Like many of Australia's
famous animals, red
kangaroos are marsupials.
Females carry their young
in their pouch. Kangaroos
move about by hopping on
their large back feet, using
their tail for balance.

Australian Rules
football

Superb
lyrebird

Sydney

Canberra

Perth

Thorny devil

Tiger shark

Melbourne

Tram

Surfer

Dugong

Blue-ringed
octopus

Whale

Tasmanian
devil

Apples

Australia

Australia is by far the biggest country in
Oceania, almost the size of the USA. More
than 22 million people live in Australia, mostly
in cities along the coasts. Most of the centre
of Australia is covered in vast stretches of hot,
dry desert, called the Outback.

The first people to live in Australia were the
Aboriginal people about 50,000 years ago.
They believe that, at the beginning of time, the
landscape was carved out by animal spirits.
Today, most Australians are descended from
European settlers.

Where is the city
of Perth?

Australia

Papua New Guinea and Solomon Islands

Papua New Guinea lies to the north of Australia. It is made up of the eastern end of the island of New Guinea. (The western end of New Guinea is part of Indonesia.) To the east are hundreds of islands, called the Solomon Islands.

There are many different groups of people in Papua New Guinea, speaking more than 800 local languages. Each group has its own style of art, dance and music. Many people are very poor. They live in small, isolated villages and farm the land.

Can you find a birdwing butterfly?

Spirit house

Clown fish

Tree kangaroo
Tree kangaroos live in the rainforests of Papua New Guinea. They are brilliant climbers, using their strong front legs to hold on to a tree trunk and their long tails for balance.

Traditional dancer

Spike-nosed tree frog

Queen Alexandra's birdwing butterfly

Port Moresby

Mud masks
At festival time, the Asaro mudmen of Papua New Guinea cover their bodies in mud and their faces with large clay masks. Traditionally, this is how they frightened off enemies.

PAPUA NEW GUINEA

Human skull

Coral reef

Pacific Ocean

Rabaul

Seashells

Volcano

Solomon Islands

Honiara

Tropical fish

House on stilts
In some parts of the Solomon Islands, people build their houses on stilts over the water. The houses are usually made of wood and thatched with palm leaves.

Coral Sea

Papua New Guinea

Solomon Islands

New Zealand and the Pacific

Tasman Sea

Kiwi fruit

Boiling mud with geyser

Auckland

Kiwi
The national emblem of New Zealand is the kiwi. About the size of a hen, it has a long beak for sniffing out food and cannot fly. It is found only in New Zealand.

Greenstone charm

NEW ZEALAND

Barracuda

Sheep

Giant tree fern

Maori dancer
The Maori were the first people to live in New Zealand more than a thousand years ago. As part of their culture, they sometimes paint their faces, and perform a war dance called a haka.

Wellington

Rock climbing

Southern Alps

Fur seals

Blue whale

Hiker

Pacific Ocean

Tuatara

Where do kiwi fruit grow?

New Zealand

Fiji

Samoa

Tonga

Vanuatu

Scattered across the southwestern Pacific Ocean lie thousands of islands. New Zealand is made up of two large islands – North and South Island – and lots of smaller ones. North and South Island are separated by the Cook Strait. North Island is warm and mild, with volcanoes and hot springs. South Island has high mountains and glaciers.

Many of the Pacific islands are the tops of volcanoes. Others are coral islands. Many islanders still live traditional lives, growing crops and fishing in the sea.

FIJI

Surfer

Angelfish

Suva

Firewalking

At special ceremonies, Fijian firewalkers, dressed as warriors, walk over burning hot stones. They practise for years beforehand, and pass their skills down through their families.

SAMOA

Apia

Bottlenose dolphin

Samoan longboat

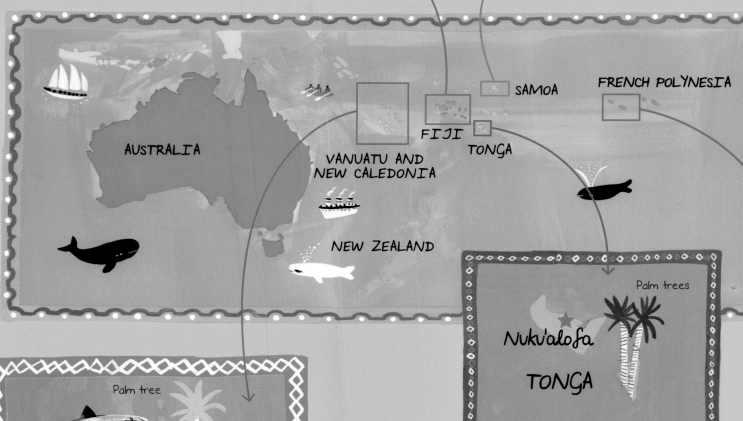

AUSTRALIA

Samoa

FRENCH POLYNESIA

FIJI

TONGA

VANUATU AND NEW CALEDONIA

NEW ZEALAND

TONGA

Palm trees

Nuku'alofa

Palm tree

Great white shark

VANUATU

Port Vila

Windsurfing

NEW CALEDONIA

Butterfly fish

Camera

Nouméa

FRENCH POLYNESIA

Lei of flowers

Pygmy orca

Papeete

Black pearls

Lobster

Tahiti

Africa

Africa is the second largest continent. It contains more than 50 countries. The biggest is Algeria, which stretches from the Mediterranean coast in the north to deep into the Sahara – the world's biggest desert – in the south. Africa has an amazing landscape. As well as desert it has rainforest in the centre, grasslands in the south and lakes and mountains along the east.

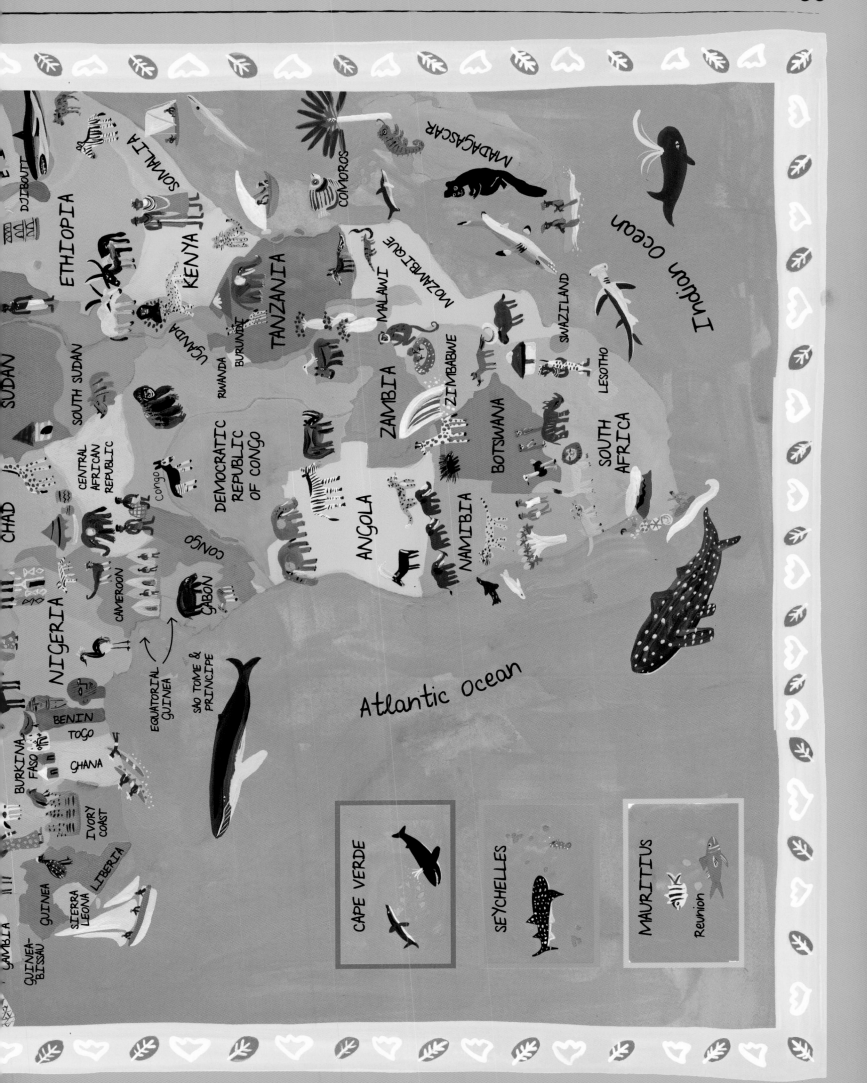

DJIBOUTI
ETHIOPIA
SOMALIA
COMOROS
MADAGASCAR
Indian Ocean

SUDAN
SOUTH SUDAN
KENYA
UGANDA
RWANDA
BURUNDI
TANZANIA
MALAWI
MOZAMBIQUE
SWAZILAND
LESOTHO

CHAD
CENTRAL AFRICAN REPUBLIC
DEMOCRATIC REPUBLIC OF CONGO
Congo
ZAMBIA
ZIMBABWE
BOTSWANA
SOUTH AFRICA

NIGERIA
CAMEROON
CONGO
GABON
ANGOLA
NAMIBIA

EQUATORIAL GUINEA
SAO TOME & PRINCIPE

BENIN
TOGO
GHANA
IVORY COAST
LIBERIA
SIERRA LEONE
GUINEA
GUINEA-BISSAU
GAMBIA
BURKINA FASO

Atlantic Ocean

CAPE VERDE

SEYCHELLES

MAURITIUS
Reunion

North and West Africa

The vast Sahara covers a large part of northern Africa. This desert can be baking hot by day and freezing cold at night. Despite these harsh conditions, many people and animals live in the desert.

The great River Nile is probably the world's longest river. It begins in Central Africa and flows north through 10 countries, including Egypt, then into the Mediterranean Sea.

Nigeria is an important country in West Africa. It has large supplies of oil and minerals, and also grows oil palms and groundnuts.

Tuareg
The Tuareg are nomads who live in the Sahara Desert. They carry goods across the desert on the back of camels. Men cover their faces with long, blue scarves to scare off evil spirits and keep out the sand.

Algiers

Rabat

Colourful rug

Roman Arch

ALGERIA

Sand dunes of the Sahara Desert

MOROCCO

Fennec fox

Dolphins

Tagine clay pot

MAURITANIA

Spoonbill

Woman with basket on head

Atlantic Ocean

Whales

Ostrich
Ostriches are the biggest birds in the world. They cannot fly but run very fast on their long legs. Ostriches eat seeds, fruit, flowers and grass. They swallow pebbles to help grind up their food.

Traditional hut

Fisherman with net

Nouakchott

MALI

Niamey

SENEGAL

Dakar

Banjul

GAMBIA

Traditional drummer

Bamako

BURKINA FASO

Flying b

Hippo swimming in ocean

GUINEA-BISSAU

Bissau

Balafon

Ouagadougou

GUINEA

IVORY COAST

GHANA

TOGO

BENIN

CAPE VERDE

Conakry

Freetown

SIERRA LEONE

Chimpanzee

Gecko

LIBERIA

Monrovia

Yamoussoukro

Necklace with gold disks

Accra

Lomé

Porto Novo

Loggerhead turtle

Leopard

Praia

Dolphin

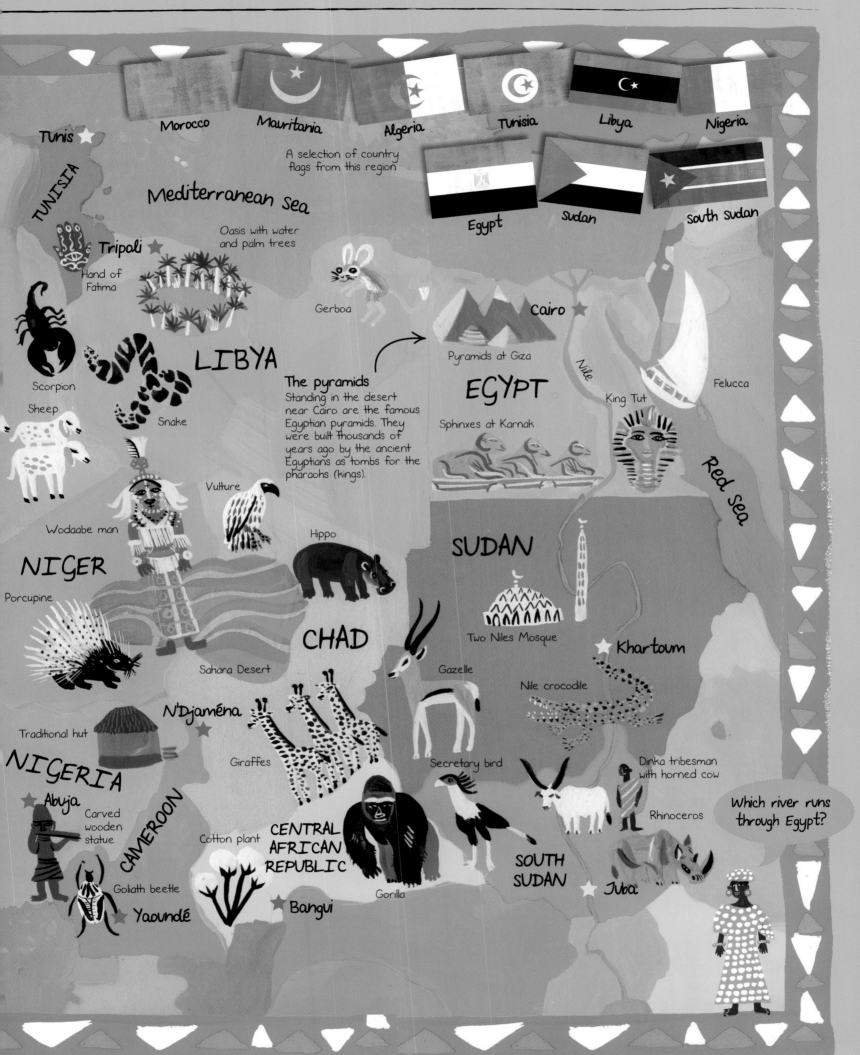

A selection of country flags from this region

Morocco
Mauritania
Algeria
Tunisia
Libya
Nigeria
Egypt
Sudan
South Sudan

Tunis
TUNISIA
Hand of Fatima
Tripoli
Mediterranean sea
Oasis with water and palm trees
Gerboa
Pyramids at Giza
Cairo
Scorpion
Sheep
Snake
LIBYA
EGYPT
Nile
King Tut
Felucca

The pyramids
Standing in the desert near Cairo are the famous Egyptian pyramids. They were built thousands of years ago by the ancient Egyptians as tombs for the pharaohs (kings).

Sphinxes at Karnak
Red Sea

Wodaabe man
Vulture
Hippo
SUDAN
NIGER
Porcupine
Two Niles Mosque
Khartoum
CHAD
Gazelle
Nile crocodile
Sahara Desert
Traditional hut
N'Djaména
Giraffes
Secretary bird
Dinka tribesman with horned cow
NIGERIA
Abuja
Carved wooden statue
CAMEROON
Cotton plant
CENTRAL AFRICAN REPUBLIC
Gorilla
SOUTH SUDAN
Rhinoceros
Goliath beetle
Yaoundé
Bangui
Juba

Which river runs through Egypt?

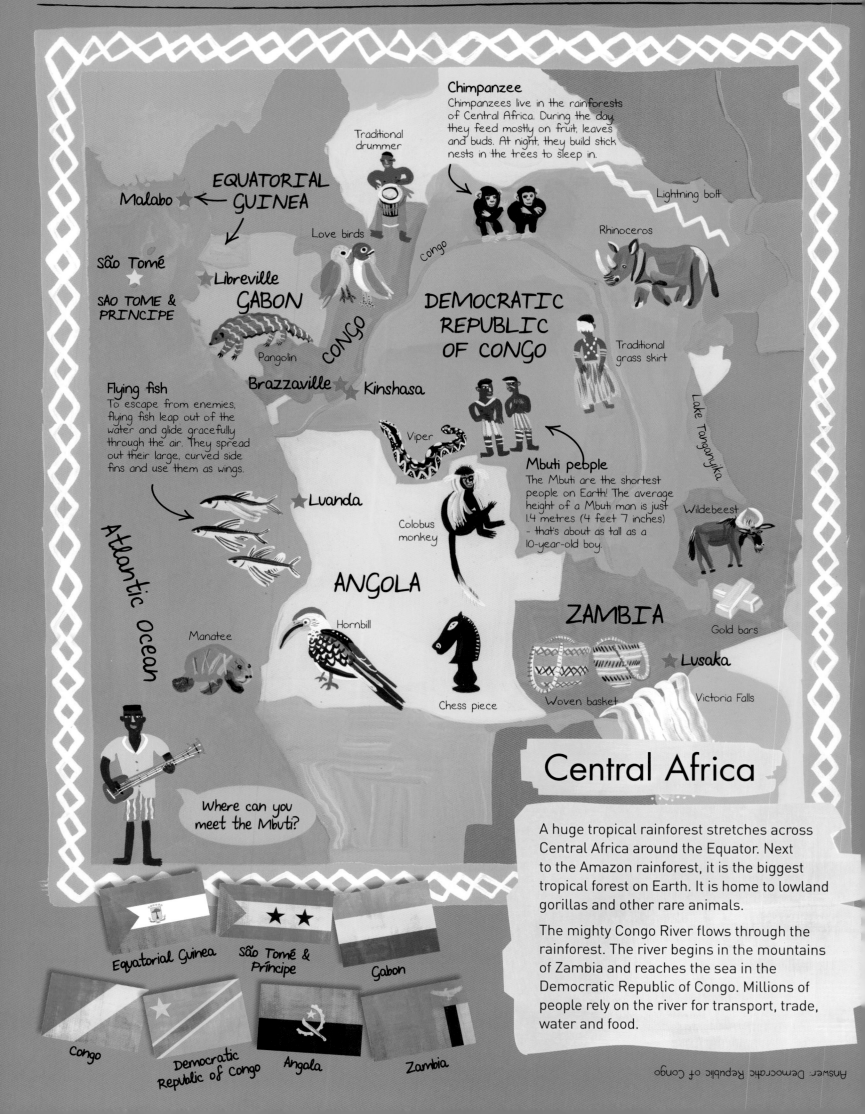

Chimpanzee
Chimpanzees live in the rainforests of Central Africa. During the day, they feed mostly on fruit, leaves and buds. At night, they build stick nests in the trees to sleep in.

Traditional drummer

Lightning bolt

EQUATORIAL GUINEA

Malabo

Rhinoceros

Love birds

São Tomé

SAO TOME & PRINCIPE

Libreville
GABON

DEMOCRATIC REPUBLIC OF CONGO

Pangolin

Congo

Traditional grass skirt

Flying fish
To escape from enemies, flying fish leap out of the water and glide gracefully through the air. They spread out their large, curved side fins and use them as wings.

Brazzaville

Kinshasa

Viper

Lake Tanganyika

Mbuti people
The Mbuti are the shortest people on Earth! The average height of a Mbuti man is just 1.4 metres (4 feet 7 inches) - that's about as tall as a 10-year-old boy.

Luanda

Colobus monkey

Wildebeest

Atlantic ocean

ANGOLA

ZAMBIA

Gold bars

Manatee

Hornbill

Lusaka

Chess piece

Woven basket

Victoria Falls

Where can you meet the Mbuti?

Central Africa

A huge tropical rainforest stretches across Central Africa around the Equator. Next to the Amazon rainforest, it is the biggest tropical forest on Earth. It is home to lowland gorillas and other rare animals.

The mighty Congo River flows through the rainforest. The river begins in the mountains of Zambia and reaches the sea in the Democratic Republic of Congo. Millions of people rely on the river for transport, trade, water and food.

Equatorial Guinea

São Tomé & Príncipe

Gabon

Congo

Democratic Republic of Congo

Angola

Zambia

Answer: Democratic Republic of Congo

East Africa

The countries of East Africa stretch from Eritrea in the north to Malawi in the south. A great crack in Earth's crust runs through the region. It is called the Great Rift Valley. A line of lakes fills the valley. There are also high mountains and volcanoes.

Kenya and Tanzania are famous for their wildlife. Huge herds of grazing animals, such as zebras and giraffes, live on the grasslands, together with lions, cheetahs and elephants. Thousands of people visit the region to go on safari – a wildlife-watching holiday.

A selection of country flags from this region

Eritrea   Ethiopia   Kenya   Tanzania

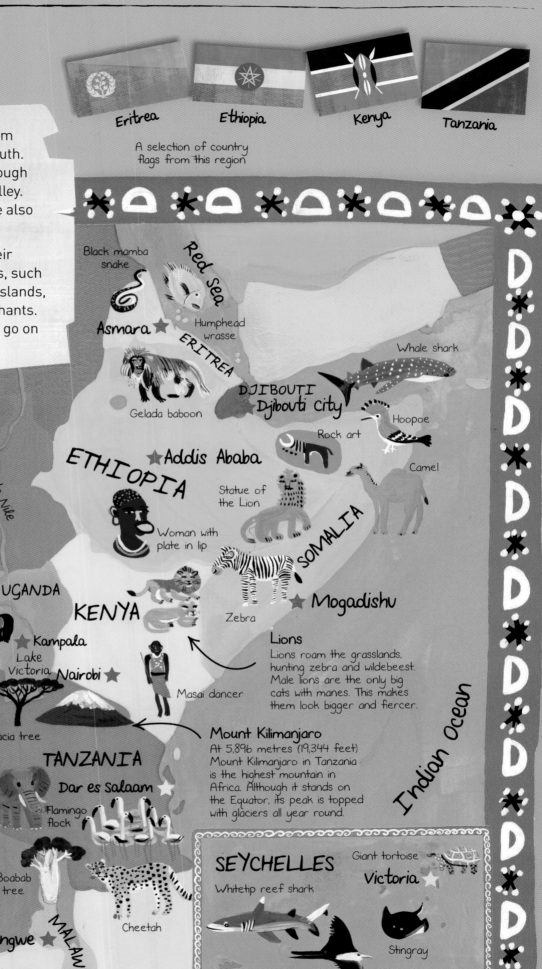

Black mamba snake

Red Sea

Asmara
ERITREA
Humphead wrasse

Whale shark

Gelada baboon

DJIBOUTI
Djibouti city

Rock art

Hoopoe

Camel

White Nile

ETHIOPIA

Addis Ababa

Woman with plate in lip

Statue of the Lion

SOMALIA

Intore dancer
Intore is a traditional dance from Rwanda. It is performed by warriors to celebrate a victory in battle. Dancers carry spears and wear long wigs made from white grasses.

Gorilla

UGANDA

KENYA

Zebra

Mogadishu

Kampala

Lake Victoria

Nairobi

Kigali

RWANDA

Bujumbura
BURUNDI

Acacia tree

Masai dancer

Lions
Lions roam the grasslands, hunting zebra and wildebeest. Male lions are the only big cats with manes. This makes them look bigger and fiercer.

Mount Kilimanjaro
At 5,896 metres (19,344 feet) Mount Kilimanjaro in Tanzania is the highest mountain in Africa. Although it stands on the Equator, its peak is topped with glaciers all year round.

TANZANIA

Elephant

Dar es Salaam

Flamingo flock

Indian Ocean

Which flag has a shield on it?

Boabab tree

Cheetah

SEYCHELLES

Whitetip reef shark

Giant tortoise

Victoria

Stingray

Frigatebird

Lilongwe

MALAWI

Answer: Kenya's

Namibia   Botswana   Zimbabwe   Swaziland   South Africa   Lesotho

Victoria Falls
The Victoria Falls is a huge waterfall on the Zambezi River where the river plunges off a cliff. Local people call it 'the smoke that thunders' because of the sound of the water crashing down.

Traditional canoe

Harare

ZIMBABWE

Ruins of Great Zimbabwe

Tribesman on stilts

Herero woman

Oryx antelope

Elephant family

NAMIBIA

Kalahari Desert

BOTSWANA

Bushman with bow and arrow

Giraffe

Aardvark

Windhoek

Meerkats

Gaborone

Zulu warrior

Maputo

Namib Desert with long sand dunes

Pretoria

Mbabane

SWAZILAND

Springbok

Safari jeep

Maseru

LESOTHO

Atlantic Ocean

Diamonds
South Africa is a world leader in diamond mining. There are seven large diamond mines in the country where diamonds are dug out of the rocks. South Africa is also rich in gold.

SOUTH AFRICA

Ndebele woman

Dugong

Cape Town

Shrimp

Great white shark

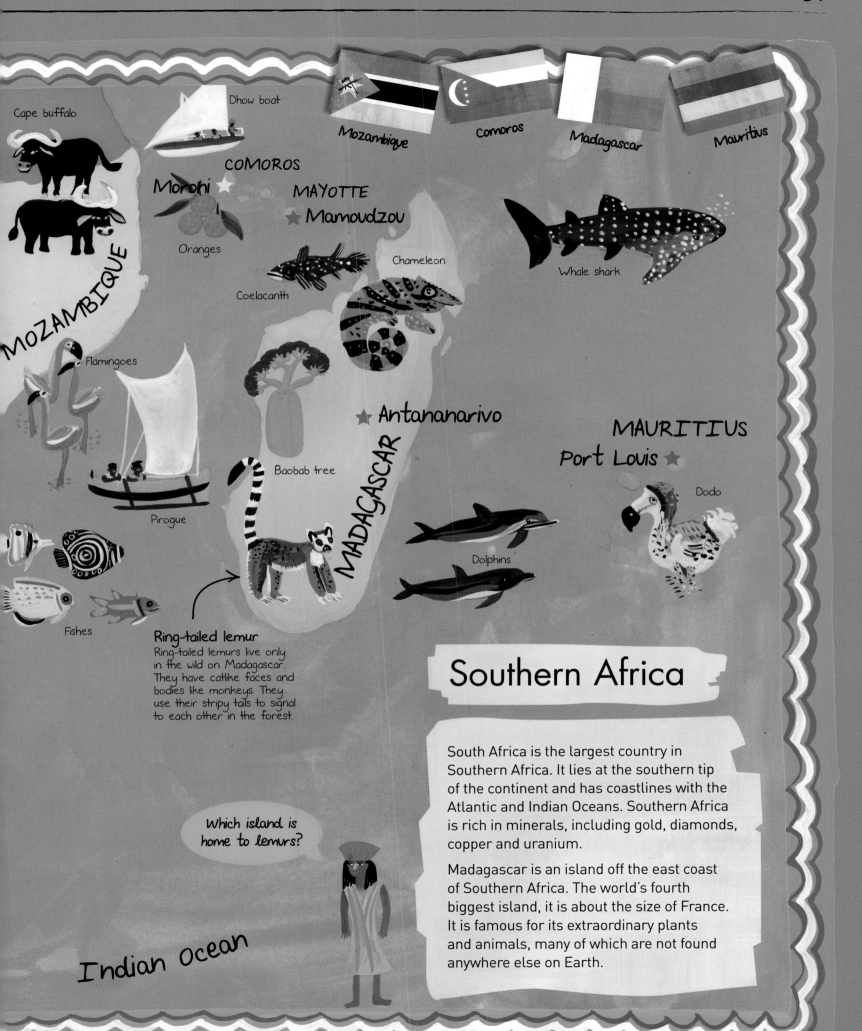

Cape buffalo

Dhow boat

Mozambique

Comoros

Madagascar

Mauritius

MOZAMBIQUE

COMOROS
Moroni ★

MAYOTTE
★ Mamoudzou

Oranges

Coelacanth

Chameleon

Whale shark

Flamingoes

Baobab tree

★ Antananarivo

MADAGASCAR

MAURITIUS
Port Louis ★

Dodo

Dolphins

Pirogue

Fishes

Ring-tailed lemur
Ring-tailed lemurs live only
in the wild on Madagascar.
They have catlike faces and
bodies like monkeys. They
use their stripy tails to signal
to each other in the forest.

Which island is
home to lemurs?

Southern Africa

South Africa is the largest country in
Southern Africa. It lies at the southern tip
of the continent and has coastlines with the
Atlantic and Indian Oceans. Southern Africa
is rich in minerals, including gold, diamonds,
copper and uranium.

Madagascar is an island off the east coast
of Southern Africa. The world's fourth
biggest island, it is about the size of France.
It is famous for its extraordinary plants
and animals, many of which are not found
anywhere else on Earth.

Indian Ocean

Answer: Madagascar

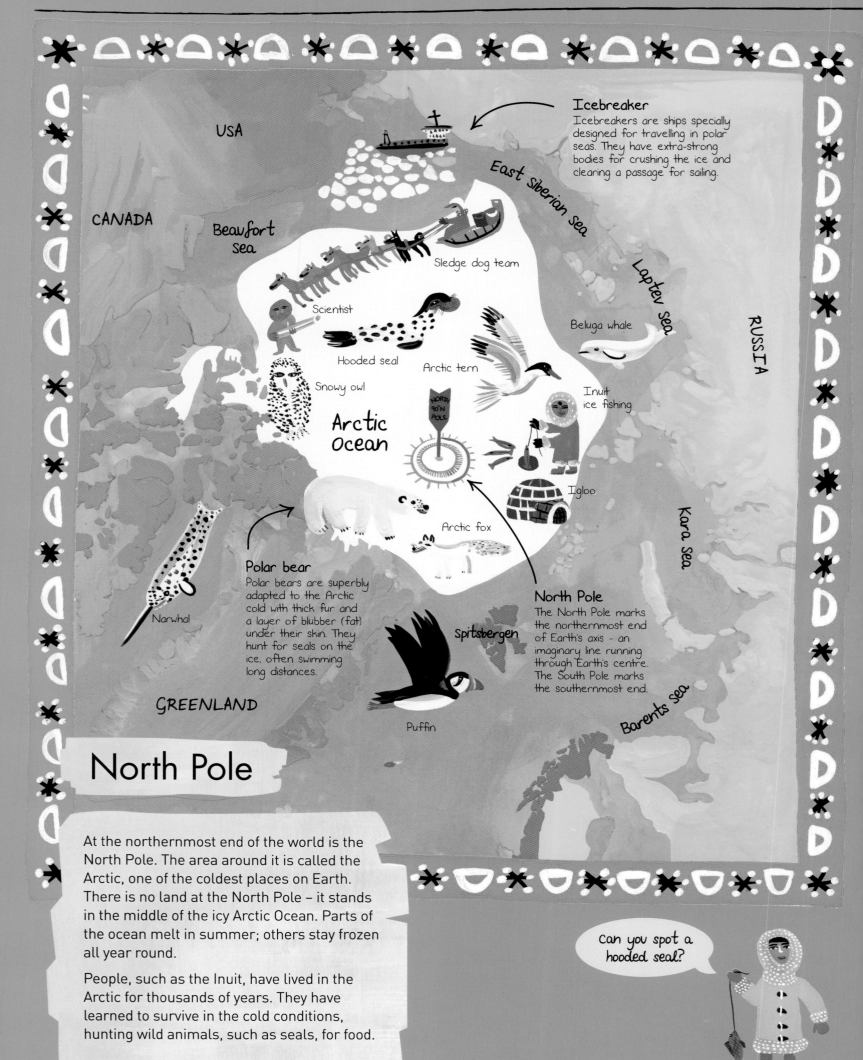

Icebreaker
Icebreakers are ships specially designed for travelling in polar seas. They have extra-strong bodies for crushing the ice and clearing a passage for sailing.

USA

CANADA

Beaufort Sea

East Siberian Sea

Laptev Sea

RUSSIA

Sledge dog team

Scientist

Beluga whale

Hooded seal

Arctic tern

Snowy owl

Inuit ice fishing

Arctic Ocean

NORTH 90°N POLE

Igloo

Arctic fox

Kara Sea

Narwhal

Polar bear
Polar bears are superbly adapted to the Arctic cold with thick fur and a layer of blubber (fat) under their skin. They hunt for seals on the ice, often swimming long distances.

North Pole
The North Pole marks the northernmost end of Earth's axis – an imaginary line running through Earth's centre. The South Pole marks the southernmost end.

Spitsbergen

GREENLAND

Puffin

Barents sea

North Pole

At the northernmost end of the world is the North Pole. The area around it is called the Arctic, one of the coldest places on Earth. There is no land at the North Pole – it stands in the middle of the icy Arctic Ocean. Parts of the ocean melt in summer; others stay frozen all year round.

People, such as the Inuit, have lived in the Arctic for thousands of years. They have learned to survive in the cold conditions, hunting wild animals, such as seals, for food.

Can you spot a hooded seal?

South Pole

How many penguins can you find?

The South Pole is in the middle of Antarctica, a continent almost twice the size of Europe. Most of Antarctica is covered in a thick sheet of ice. Buried beneath the ice are mountains, valleys and volcanoes. Antarctica is surrounded by the stormy Southern Ocean. In winter, some of the sea freezes, doubling the size of the continent.

The only people on Antarctica are scientists from countries around the world. They live on bases dotted across the continent and study the unique climate, ice, landscape and wildlife.

Southern Ocean

Emperor penguins
Emperor penguins breed on the ice during the freezing Antarctic winter. For months the males huddle together, guarding their eggs. They hold them on the top of their feet to keep them off the ice.

Humpback whale

Wandering albatross

Weddell sea

ANTARCTICA

Ski plane

Giant squid

Cruise ship

Snow tractor

Scientist in snowsuit

south Pole

Leopard seal

Skua

Mt Erebus volcano

South Pole
The United States' Amundsen-Scott research base stands at the South Pole. It is named after two of the greatest polar explorers ever. In summer, the base is home to 200 scientists.

Rockhopper penguins

Ice shelf
Enormous shelves of ice stretch out to sea. Huge chunks of ice break off the shelves to form icebergs. In places, the ice shelves are also melting as the world is getting warmer.

Ross sea

Icebergs

Macaroni penguins with colourful crests

Krill

Orcas

Southern Ocean

Blue whale

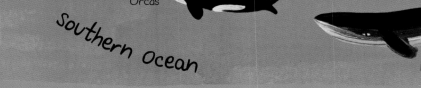

Arctic Ocean

NORTH POLE ↗

NORTH
AMERICA

Pacific Ocean

Atlantic Ocean

North Se

Caribbean Sea

SOUTH
AMERICA

Atlantic Ocean

The World

Planet Earth, the world we live on, is one of eight planets that circle around the Sun. More than two-thirds of our world is covered in water – in the oceans, seas, rivers and lakes. The rest is dry land, divided into seven main chunks, called continents. These are Asia, Africa, North America, South America, Antarctica, Europe and Australia. On these continents there are hundreds of different countries.

SOUTH POLE ↘

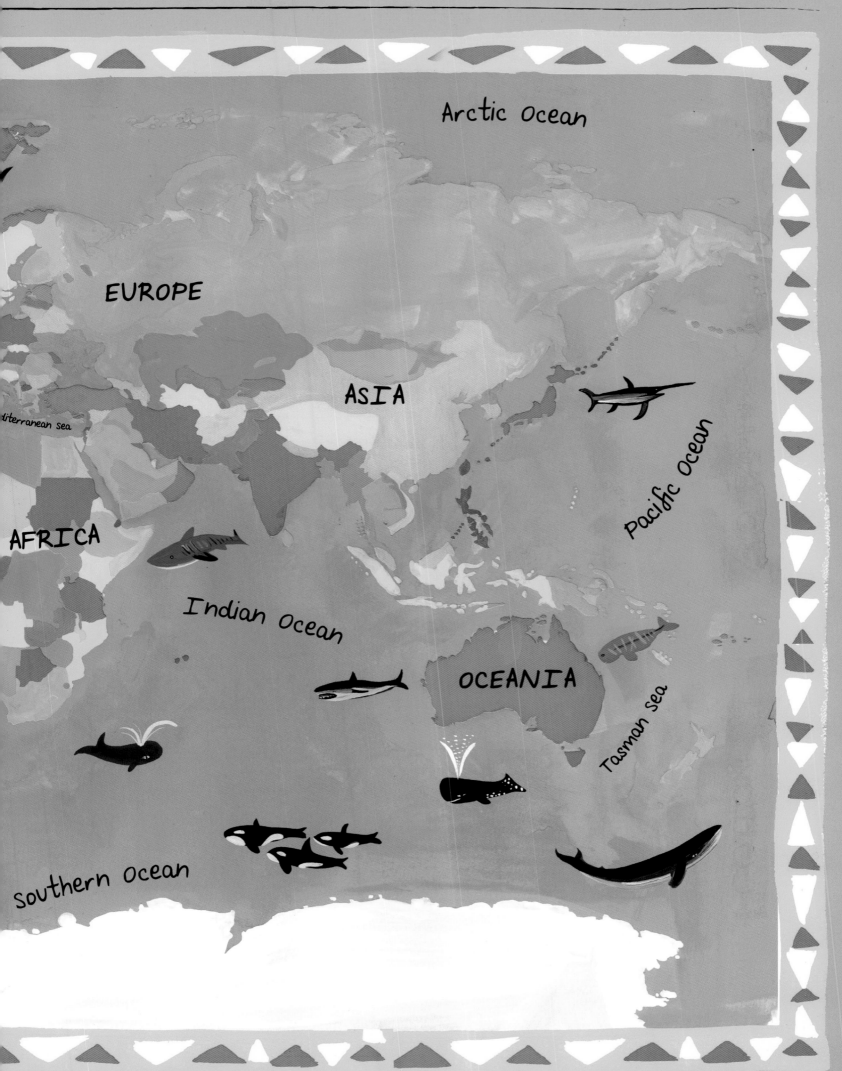

Arctic Ocean

EUROPE

ASIA

Mediterranean sea

AFRICA

Pacific Ocean

Indian Ocean

OCEANIA

Tasman Sea

Southern Ocean

Index

Afghanistan 38
Albania 29
Algeria 54–55
Andorra 23
Angola 56
Antarctica 61
Antigua & Barbuda 11
Arctic, The 60
Argentina 16–17
Armenia 34
Australia 48
Austria 25
Azerbaijan 34
Bahamas 10
Bahrain 35
Bangladesh 39
Barbados 11
Belarus 30
Belgium 24
Belize 9
Benin 54
Bhutan 39
Bolivia 16
Bosnia & Hercegovina 27
Botswana 58
Brazil 15
Brunei 44
Bulgaria 26
Burkina Faso 54
Burundi 57
Cambodia 40
Cameroon 55
Canada 7
Cape Verde 54
Central African Republic 55
Chad 55
Chile 16–17
China 41
Colombia 14
Comoros & Mayotte 59
Congo 56
Costa Rica 9
Croatia 27
Cuba 10
Cyprus 34
Czech Republic 26
Democratic Republic of Congo 56
Denmark 20
Djibouti 57
Dominica 11
Dominican Republic 11
East Timor 45
Ecuador 14

Egypt 55
El Salvador 9
England 21
Equatorial Guinea 56
Eritrea 57
Estonia 30
Ethiopia 57
Federated States of Micronesia 47
Fiji 51
Finland 20
France 23
French Guiana 15
French Polynesia 51
Gabon 56
Gambia 54
Georgia 34
Germany 25
Ghana 54
Greece 29
Greenland 7
Grenada 11
Guatemala 9
Guinea 54
Guinea-Bissau 54
Guyana 15
Haiti 10
Honduras 9
Hungary 26
Iceland 7
India 39
Indonesia 44–45
Iran 35
Iraq 35
Ireland 21
Israel 34
Italy 28
Ivory Coast 54
Jamaica 10
Japan 43
Jordan 34
Kazakhstan 36–37
Kenya 57
Kiribati 47
Kosovo 27
Kuwait 35
Kyrgyzstan 37
Laos 40
Latvia 30
Lebanon 34
Lesotho 58
Liberia 54
Libya 55
Liechtenstein 25

Lithuania 30
Luxembourg 24
Macedonia 29
Madagascar 59
Malawi 57
Malaysia 44
Maldives 39
Mali 54
Malta 28
Marshall Islands 47
Mauritania 54
Mauritius 59
Mayotte 59
Mexico 8–9
Moldova 30
Monaco 23
Mongolia 41
Montenegro 27
Morocco 54
Mozambique 58–59
Myanmar 40
Namibia 58
Nauru 47
Nepal 39
Netherlands 24
New Caledonia 51
New Zealand 50
Nicaragua 9
Niger 54–55
Nigeria 54–55
North Korea 42
Northern Ireland 21
Norway 20
Oman 35
Pakistan 38
Palau 46
Palestine 34
Panama 9
Papua New Guinea 49
Paraguay 16
Peru 14
Philippines 45
Poland 26
Portugal 22
Puerto Rico 11
Qatar 35
Romania 26
Russia 30–31
Rwanda 57
Saint Kitts & Nevis 11
Saint Lucia 11
Saint Vincent & the Grenadines 11
Samoa 51

San Marino 28
São Tomé & Príncipe 56
Saudi Arabia 35
Scotland 21
Senegal 54
Serbia 27
Seychelles 57
Sierra Leone 54
Singapore 44
Slovakia 26
Slovenia 27
Solomon Islands 49
Somalia 57
South Africa 58
South Korea 42
South Sudan 55
Spain 22
Sri Lanka 39
Sudan 55
Suriname 15
Swaziland 58
Sweden 20
Switzerland 25
Syria 34
Taiwan 41
Tajikistan 37
Tanzania 57
Thailand 40
Tibet 41
Togo 54
Tonga 51
Trinidad & Tobago 11
Tunisia 55
Turkey 34
Turkmenistan 36
Tuvalu 47
Uganda 57
Ukraine 30
United Arab Emirates 35
United Kingdom 21
United States of America 6
Uruguay 16
Uzbekistan 36–37
Vanuatu 51
Vatican City 28
Venezuela 14
Vietnam 40
Virgin Islands 11
Wales 21
Yemen 35
Zambia 56
Zimbabwe 58

Published by WeldonOwen Publishing
42–44 Victoria Street, McMahons Point
Sydney NSW 2060, Australia
weldonowenpublishing.com

Copyright © 2012 Weldon Owen Pty Ltd

WeldonOwen PUBLISHING

Managing Director Kay Scarlett
Publisher Corinne Roberts
Creative Director Sue Burk
Senior Vice President, International Sales Stuart Laurence
Sales Manager, North America Ellen Towell
Administration Manager, International Sales Kristine Ravn
Managing Editor Averil Moffat
Senior Editor Barbara McClenahan
Designer Maria Harding/Colourful Ideas
Illustrations Christopher Corr
Images Manager Trucie Henderson
Production Director Todd Rechner
Production and Prepress Controller Mike Crowton

ISBN: 978-1-74252-279-1

Printed and bound in China by 1010 Printing Int Ltd

The paper used in the manufacture of this book is sourced from wood grown in sustainable forests. It complies with the Environmental Management System Standard ISO 14001:2004